Libraries and Archives

Design and Renovation with a Preservation Perspective

Susan Garretson Swartzburg
and Holly Bussey
with Frank Garretson

The Scarecrow Press, Inc.
Lanham, Maryland, & London
1998

SCARECROW PRESS, INC.

Published in the United States of America
by Scarecrow Press, Inc.
4720 Boston Way
Lanham, Maryland 20706

4 Pleydell Gardens, Folkestone
Kent CT20 2DN, England

Copyright © 1991 by Susan Garretson Swartzburg and Holly Bussey
First paperback printing 1998

British Library Cataloguing in Publication Information Available

Library of Congress Cataloging-in-Publication Data

Swartzburg, Susan G., 1938–1996.
    Libraries and archives : design and renovation with a
preservation perspective / by Susan Garretson Swartzburg
and Holly Bussey, with Frank Garretson.
        p.   cm.
    Includes bibliographical references and indexes.
    ISBN 0-8108-3560-6 (alk. paper)

    1. Library architecture.   2. Library materials—
Conservation and restoration.   3. Archive buildings.
4. Archival materials—Conservation and restoration.
I. Bussey, Holly, 1954–   II. Garretson, Frank.
III. Title.
Z679.S84   1991
727'.8—dc20   91-24415
                                            CIP

This book is dedicated to Professor
Thomas Hezekiah Mott, Jr., 1924-1989,
in appreciation for his support and
his friendship.

Contents

Preface

THE TEXT AND BIBLIOGRAPHIES for this book grew out of a project that began in 1980 with a review of the literature on library design and renovation, in preparation for the construction of an annex to house infrequently used research and archival collections of the Rutgers University Libraries. As research progressed, it was evident that in spite of a large body of literature on the design of library and archive buildings, much of it was of little practical value. Further, the majority of the literature was not concerned with the physical environment appropriate for the housing of library and archival collections.

The need was obvious for a selective bibliography to focus on design that would not only house collections appropriately but also be comfortable for readers and staff. Holly Bussey, as a graduate student at the School of Communication, Information and Library Studies, Rutgers University, had prepared a bibliography on the planning and design of archival repositories, and together we began an exhaustive review of the published literature published in the United States and abroad. We enlisted the collaboration of architect and architectural historian Frank M. Garretson to provide a technical and historical perspective.

As we worked on the book, we discussed at length the impact of new technologies on the planning and construction of library and archive buildings. However, it was the collapse of a section of the bookstacks in the Rutgers Library Annex and in the New Jersey State Archives and Records Center, each employing the same new shelving technology, that brought home the implications of the use of new materials and methods of construction, their dangers as well as their advantages. In the bibliographies, we have attempted to cite books and articles that will provoke thought about new technologies and materials, with the understanding that the only way to keep abreast of the rapidly changing field of building technology is by careful attention to the literature; major journals are cited in Appendix III. Key citations are starred (*).

When planning a library or archive repository, the architect needs to select materials and methods of construction that are appropriate for the use that the collections are to receive in the environment where they are located. Although one must consider the use of new construction technologies with the greatest care, one cannot reject them out of hand because of the disaster at Rutgers or another institution. One must proceed with some knowledge of design and construction, common sense, and an awareness that there will be many "glitches" before a project is completed. The goal is to catch them as quickly as possible and remedy them. The carefully prepared administrator will be able to do so.

We would like to thank the people who have contributed their time and expertise to help make this book successful. Paul N. Banks, School of Library Service, Columbia University; Albert Brady, Physical Plant, Rutgers University; Christopher Campbell, consultant, formerly University Safety Engineer, Rutgers University; Beryl Smith, Assistant Art Librarian, Rutgers University Library; and Richard Strassberg, Cornell University. Each read the manuscript and offered a number of suggestions to strengthen and clarify the text. Colleagues at Rutgers, Ilona Caparros, George Kanzler and Neha Weinstein, and Danielle Mihram, University of Southern California Library, assisted with translations. We could not have completed the project, which involved the review of so much material, without the patience and support of the circulation, reference and document delivery personnel at Rutgers University Libraries.

The students at the School of Communication, Information and Library Studies, Rutgers University, have provided considerable assistance over the past eight years.

We especially want to acknowledge the contribution of Jacquelin Miller in the preparation of the section on security. Research assistants Pat Buickerood and Cathy Weglarz tracked many an elusive reference and coped with innumerable inter-library loan requests.

Neha Weinstein, Edwin P. Garretson and Suzette André devoted many hours to editing and proofreading the manuscript. We were assisted in the final review by Marshall and Mark Swartzburg, both of whom are skilled bibliographical detectives. Dorothy and Al Bussey and Holly's husband, James Sanders, who became a spouse "right in the middle of all this work," lent encouragement and support through it all.

We especially want to remember the late Professor Thomas Hezekiah Mott, Jr., of Rutgers University, for his support, encouragement, and sound advice throughout this project; we regret that he did not live to see the final product. It is to him that we dedicate this book.

Susan G. Swartzburg
Holly J. Bussey
Frank M. Garretson

June 1991

PART ONE:

THE DESIGN OF LIBRARIES AND THE PRESERVATION OF BOOKS

A Summary History

I. EARLY LIBRARIES

FROM THE BEGINNINGS of human society, libraries have existed as collections of materials for the communication of information. In *The Beginnings of Libraries*, Ernest Cushing Richardson observes that all definitions of a library "imply a book or books, a place of keeping and somebody to do the keeping . . . some emphasize the books, some the place and some the keeping."[1] The earliest "libraries" were collections of symbolic drawings inscribed on the walls of caves (such as those found in Lascaux in France) or upon skins, bark, bones, bamboo, shell or other materials receptive to marking. Objects, such as wampum, were designed in patterns that had a particular meaning for the people who consulted them. Information was inscribed on stone surfaces and upon clay tablets. "The very simplest library consists . . . of a single recorded sign kept for use. It is the feeble first beginning of a library but just as much a library as the New York Public Library, the Library of Congress, the British Museum, or the Bibliotheque Nationale."[2]

Although the earliest collections were probably religious in nature, the symbols used represented the basics of human existence: man, woman, home. These symbols evolved into the written word. Because sacred records were highly valued by ancient societies, they were kept in the best possible environment, such as a cave, or, later, a temple.

People have always recognized the informational value of their records and the need to preserve them with great care. Albertine Gaur of the British Library writes, "All

3

writing is information storage. It is not the only form of information storage. Long before, and in many cases, simultaneously with it, human memory served the same purpose. . . . If all writing is information storage, then all writing is of equal value. Each society stores the information essential to its survival, the information which enables it to function effectively."[3]

Gaur continues, "Most codified forms of writing using phonetic elements developed . . . between 4000-3000 B.C. in the Near East, in Mesopotamia and in Egypt, the region known as the Fertile Crescent."[4] It was there that the earliest archives, or libraries, as we recognize them today, were established. They contained the temporal records of a mercantile society, a collection of information documenting almost every aspect of everyday life. The preservation of that information was of great importance to the Mediterranean cultures. Materials such as clay tablets and, later, papyrus were devised especially for writing.

Buildings were constructed to house these written materials. Great care was taken to ensure that records were protected in safe, secure conditions. Historian and archivist Ernst Posner writes, "A system of organization and administration that can truly be called bureaucratic, and the cheapness and availability of writing materials— both lacking in the Middle Ages—resulted in a mass production of records on clay and papyrus that created preservation problems similar to those confronting the archivist in the age of paper."[5] Public records, literary works, even household records, were collected and preserved. Clay tablets offered an excellent medium for preservation—over 400,000 of them have survived from the second millennium B.C. until today. They were carefully arranged and stored in specially designed and labeled clay containers housed in the library/archive. Clay tablets were susceptible to atmospheric conditions, and unbaked tablets could crumble in the hot Mediterranean climate. To provide a more desirable humidity level, the archive storage area in the Mesopotamian city of Uruk had a grooved floor so that water could flow and evaporate, an excellent method of controlling temperature and humidity.[6] The clay containers were placed on wooden shelves on the floor or on clay banquettes.[7]

The Egyptians developed a bureaucratic structure of government in which records played a highly important role. Posner observes, "Appreciation of the records was forced upon the entire people and penetrated into their thinking."[8] The scribes who wrote and preserved the records of Egyptian society were among its most important officials. Papyrus, a cheaply produced writing material made from the reed-like papyrus plant that grew prolifically in the Nile delta, was the principal material used for the keeping of records. The earliest extant papyrus fragments are from temple account books written in the Fifth Dynasty, circa 2494-2345 B.C.[9] Papyrus has proven to be remarkably durable when it has been stored under good conditions.

Remains of Egyptian archives have not survived, but it is known that there were central records repositories as well as smaller ones for administrative departments. Many records were also stored in temples, as religion and government were intimately intertwined. Texts were written on rolls of papyrus and stored in wooden chests or clay jars. These rolls were also stored in niches or pigeonholes, a practice that became common in Roman society. Posner postulates that, given the bureaucratic nature of Egyptian society, procedures for weeding collections "were not even contemplated." However, unnecessary papyrus sheets which could be reused were clandestinely disposed of, usually to the undertakers, "who used strips of papyrus for stuffing and wrapping the corpses during the process of mummification."[10] Some of this material has survived until today, providing a glimpse of the records that documented everyday life in the Nile delta.

Leather and skins were also used for written records, although these have not survived as well. Skins were used as a medium for writing from the earliest times, but parchment, the skin of sheep, did not come into use until the reign of Eumenes II of Pergamum in Asia Minor (197-158 B.C.). Parchment did not begin to rival papyrus as a writing medium until the second century A.D. Leather, such as parchment, is not as permanent a medium as papyrus.

Few remains of Greek libraries survive, and our knowledge of them is derived from literary sources. The papyrus roll, probably in use in Greece by the middle of the seventh century B.C., was employed to transcribe the literature of the Greeks as well as their everyday records. Clay, wax tablets and boards were used as well. The book trade flourished in Athens by the middle of the fifth century B.C.[11] Because the Greeks considered personal records to be semi-public property, their libraries contained both public and personal records as well as literary material. Records that were considered to be of a permanent nature were incised in stone, as had been done in Mesopotamia. The need for a repository to house archival records was recognized in Athens in the late fifth century, and special buildings for the purpose were erected on the Acropolis. Records were probably stored in chests and jars, or rolled in niches, as they were in Egyptian libraries. The preservation of the records of society and its literature were important to the Greeks, but their climate did not provide the favorable conditions for long-term preservation found in the dryer regions of Asia Minor and Egypt.

The Egyptian tradition of bureaucratic order carried into the Greco-Roman period. Much is known about the great libraries in Alexandria and Pergamum although they did not survive. More is known about Roman libraries since many of their buildings have survived. The Tabularium, the state archives building of Rome, was built in 75 B.C. It connected two separate hills and provided "an imposing terminal point to the Forum."[12] Posner has written, "For the first time in the history of mankind, a monumental and fire-resistive structure for housing the state's archives was erected,"[13] a repository that also reflected the glory that was Rome. The main storage area was destroyed during the barbarian invasions, so the precise method of storing archival materials is not known. There is, however, ample documentary evidence to show that great care was taken in the arrangement and storage of the collection.

The first "public" library, which contained both Greek and Latin literature, was established by Asinius Pollio in 37 B.C., during the reign of Augustus. The classical design of the building has served as a model of library design to the present time, reflecting the importance of the library as a public structure. A temple dedicated to Apollo was in the center of the building; wings containing the collections of Greek and Roman works were on either side.

Private libraries in the homes of the wealthy flourished, and quixotic collecting habits were as common then as they are today. Collections, both public and private, were not only meant to reflect the learning and wisdom of the collector, but also his esteemed role in Roman society. Roll and codex were carefully housed in niches or upon shelves in beautifully decorated rooms. The codex format of the book developed in the first century A.D. and slowly superceded the rolled book because it was a far more convenient format for storing and handling. Presses, enclosed cabinets, became more common in the second century since they could better accommodate the storage of codexes.

The model of the Roman library carried into its empire, although these libraries and their contents died from neglect and continuous pilfering during the empire's decline. Neither the early Christians nor the barbarian invaders were concerned with books and learning in the Dark Ages. As the secular society disintegrated, learning and books moved to the Church and the monasteries, where the preservation of the writings of the Church fathers was emphasized. Books became precious objects: neither writing materials nor people who could copy books were readily available. Books were accumulated in the monastery and transcribed by literate monks in the scriptorium. Library historian James Westfall Thompson notes, "The separation of library from scriptorium and the evolution of a specially equipped bookroom were both gradual processes; and, indeed, the final phase was never reached in many monasteries."[14] Cassiodorus, a Roman noble and scholar of the sixth century, established the rules for the copying of manuscripts that carried through the Middle Ages. Florence Edler de Roover notes that copying by artificial light was usually not permitted because of the greater possibility of mistakes in transcription and also because of the danger to the precious manuscripts from grease or fire.[15]

Monastic and church libraries sprang up throughout the Holy Roman Empire during and following the Carolingian Renaissance of the ninth century. The preservation of books was considered an important mission. Each monastic order decreed its own rules for the care, storage and distribution of books. Librarian Francis Wormald writes, "Books were read and kept in three places . . . by far the most usual arrangement was for the books to be kept in cupboards [presses] in the cloister, usually on the side nearest the church. If other accommodation was necessary, it appears that rooms off the cloister were used as book stores and not as libraries. If the monks were to have any special place to work it would be in the carrels in the cloister."[16]

Great attention was paid to the storage of books because of their value. Library historian J.W. Clark, in his study, *The Observances in Use at the Augustinian Priory of Barnwell*, writes, "The books themselves were placed in cupboards, which, according to the Barnwell Customs, ought to be lined inside with wood, so that the walls might not moisten or stain the books. These presses . . . should be divided vertically as well as horizontally by sundry shelves on which the books may be ranged so as to be separate from one another, for fear they may be packed so close as to injure each other or delay those who want them."[17]

With the rise of a literate secular society and the development of universities, books became more plentiful. The invention of paper made its way west from China, and the first paper mills were established in Europe by the late twelfth century. Paper became a less expensive medium for writing, although it was recognized that paper was not a stable, permanent medium for written records.

The early universities occasionally had rooms that housed collections of books, but the development of academic libraries was slow. Clark has observed, "Erection of a library proper was an afterthought in many of the older colleges, as it was in the monasteries."[18] Collegiate libraries were "derived from monastic Customs, using the word in its technical sense, and monastic practice."[19] Collections were small and books were valuable. The loss of even one volume from a collection was serious. Rules for the use of a university's collection of books were drawn up to ensure the safe return of materials. Like the monks before them, students were often allowed one, possibly two, books from the collection at a time, and that time period was usually for one year.

Because of the need for use and the need for security, a lectern system of housing the books in the library evolved in the thirteenth century. Volumes were chained to stalls and rested on their sloping sides; study carrels were attached. The texts themselves were attached by a chain to a bar that was locked in but which could be opened if a book was to be removed. This system presented problems for the readers and even greater problems for the volumes themselves. Their textblocks were damaged because of the slope of the shelf and the weight of the chain. Thus, the stall system evolved. Books were housed on shelves in stalls with a working area attached, in a manner similar to the study carrel of today. Although the books were chained, the stall system allowed the users more room and provided far more support for the books themselves.

The libraries were housed in a "long, narrow room lighted by rows of equidistant windows."[20] Windows were a necessity for ventilation and light for reading. Today the library environment can be controlled by mechanical means. And, although the harmful effect of light upon library materials is well known, library designers too frequently continue to follow a medieval plan for library design.

By the fifteenth century, the spirit of the Renaissance, a

rebirth of learning and a turning to the knowledge of the "ancients," had swept northward from Italy throughout the Holy Roman Empire. In his study *The Architecture of the Monastic Library in Italy, 1300-1600*, historian James F. O'Gorman writes, "The monastic library marked the confluence of these two Renaissance passions, architecture and learning, and was therefore a most important architectural problem."[21] Renaissance libraries reaffirmed the Greco-Roman tradition of the library as monument to its patron. The monastic libraries, supported by princely patrons, grew in wealth. Many existing library buildings were redesigned and expanded by the greatest architects of the period. Beautiful new libraries were designed for princes, monasteries and scholars. The basilical form superceded the long, narrow hall that was common through the fourteenth century. The library was frequently located on the second story of a building, with the scriptorium on the entry level, following the model at St. Gall. An advantage of the design is graphically illustrated by photographs of the library of the Santa Croce Monastery in Florence taken before and just following the flood of the Arno River in November 1966. When they planned the library, the monks realized that, given the history of the Arno, a first floor location for the library would not be satisfactory.

The Vatican Library, reflecting the Renaissance in all of its glory, was built between 1471 and 1475. Careful records were kept of all expenditures, documenting the purchase of supplies for binding and book repair. Juniper was used for fumigation, brooms were used to clean the library, and fox-tails were used for dusting the books, which were shelved in cabinets and stalls.[22]

With the proliferation of printing presses and a more plentiful supply of paper, the publication of books became an economical, often profitable, undertaking. Library collections—private, university, church, and state—were developed at a rapid rate. Libraries continued to be built to reflect the glory of their owners. The great Baroque libraries of Europe, such as the monastic library at Melk and the Austrian National Library in Vienna, were built between 1600 and 1800. These buildings are "at once dramatic, rich, grand and alive; architecture, sculpture, painting and craft all were used in harmony to produce a unified whole."[23] Because the interiors were meant to be dramatic, great care was taken to control natural light. Concealed windows directed light to specific points in the architecture. Books were placed in shelves around the perimeter of the room, away from direct light. The windows were usually small, following the dictates of climate. A return to the neo-classical style, a style of greater simplicity, occurred during the eighteenth century, the age of enlightenment and rationality, which carried into the nineteenth century.

The Bibliothèque Sainte-Geneviève in Paris, erected between 1843 and 1850, had enormous impact on library design in Europe and America. Designed by Pierre-François-Henri Labrouste (1801-1875), it was the first French library to be planned as a separate building. Labrouste believed that the elements of architecture "are modified according to the functions they are made to serve and thus demand the selection of materials most appropriate for enabling them to satisfy these functions."[24] He made use of new materials and new methods of technology in the design of the library. Inside its stone shell was a complete iron frame which ran from top to bottom, surmounted by a metal double roof. Its outer iron pillars were embedded in its masonry walls. Labrouste's use of the iron frame enabled him to create a library which housed its less frequently used materials in a closed stack area on the ground floor, whereas the remainder of the books were placed around the walls of the single long reading room above. The library was lit by gaslight and thus its structure was meant to be fireproof. The system devised was lightweight and could be erected quickly.

In 1854 Labrouste was chosen to be the architect of the Bibliothèque Nationale, which was built between 1860 and 1867. It has been described as "a small skyscraper building."[25] Labrouste designed bookstacks that were "a tightly fitted cage of iron shelves and glass platforms, the first of the now familiar type ever erected."[26] For its day, it was a sensible solution for the housing of ever-expanding book collections in a way that made them accessible. This structure became the model for most libraries constructed in Europe and America until 1930. However, safety and security specialist John Morris has recently pointed out that this structure is, ironically, particularly vulnerable to fire because the open stairways and open slots in the floors of the stacks will carry heat and smoke upward, like a flue, and the light metal support structure will quickly buckle.[27] The Los Angeles Public Library is similar in design; had it not been for heroic firefighting and luck, the entire building and its collections would have been lost when it was set afire in 1985.[28] Many existing libraries are designed following the Labrouste model, which was advocated by American library planners early in the century. The Los Angeles fire was a sobering experience. The renovation of these libraries will be difficult and costly.

Until this century, the care of the materials within library and archive repositories was the primary concern of librarians and archivists. Buildings were planned with the collections in mind. There were fewer users, and their intent was more likely to be scholarly than informational. It is not surprising that American librarians, in an egalitarian society, were more anxious than their European counterparts to address the needs of the patron, an ever-expanding, ever more literate public eager to devour the contents of the books that were pouring from the mechanized presses.

II. DEVELOPMENT OF AMERICAN LIBRARIES

The spirit of independence that fostered literacy and libraries reached America with its first settlers. The desire to acquire, organize, preserve and make available the written word was one of the foundations upon which the country was built. The colonists planned libraries, from the first settlement in Jamestown to the establishment of Harvard in 1639. By the middle of the eighteenth century, libraries were established in Philadelphia, Newport, New York, Charleston and the other important colonial cities as well as in the newly established colleges. The first American library building was erected in Newport, Rhode Island, in 1750. Designed by Peter Harrison (1716-1775), America's first architect, the Redwood Library was a Palladian building based upon the popular English style of the period.

A period of extraordinary development for libraries in America occurred between 1850 and 1970. At the beginning, the great European libraries, discussed earlier in this section, provided models toward which the Americans could and did aspire. The first American architectural program was established in 1868 by William Robert Ware (1832-1915) at the Massachusetts Institute of Technology. Ware moved on to establish the department at Columbia University in 1881.[29] The architectural profession was becoming organized, and professional standards were of great concern. At the same time, there was a need for library buildings, both public and academic.

Justin Winsor (1831-1897), librarian of Harvard College and the first president of the American Library Association, recognized the shortcomings of the alcove system, based upon the European model, which was popular in most libraries.[30] In an article, "Library Buildings," published as a part of a special report, *Public Libraries in the United States of America*, issued by the Bureau of Education in 1876, he wrote that the alcove system had "come down to us with other monastic ideas, when the monks were the only users of books; when the seclusion of the alcoves comported with their literary habits."[31] Winsor advocated a separation of books and readers; books were to be stored compactly a short distance from the readers to save space. Winsor implemented this concept at the Roxbury Branch Library in Boston in 1872-73.

Working with Ware, Winsor was able to put his ideas into practice with the design of the addition to Gore Hall, the Harvard College Library. By 1825 Harvard College Library boasted 25,000 volumes. Gore Hall, Harvard's first library building, was built in 1841 based upon the alcove model. By 1877 it was inadequate to contain the steady flow of acquisitions.[32] Ware and Winsor designed a shell of masonry walls pierced by rows of small windows and topped by a truss system and roofing, echoing the influence of Labrouste. The library is thus described:

> Into this were packed book ranges, row on row, tier on tier, with only enough vacant space to give access to the books. The aisles between the ranges were 28 inches wide and tiers seven feet high, allowing the topmost of the seven rows of shelves to be easily reached. The stack was six tiers high, self supporting throughout, and depended on the building for protection only. The vertical shelf support walls were of cast iron open work, the deck framing of rolled wrought iron, the deck flooring of perforated cast iron slabs and the shelves of wood, supported at the ends by light zinc Z bars fitting into notches in the uprights.[33]

This construction was a major advance in compact permanent shelving at a time when the increase in book production required a solution to the problem of rapidly expanding book collections. It was widely copied and, in modified form, continues to be a major style of bookstack construction today. One advantage, from the preservation perspective, is that it discourages casual browsing and thus protects, to some extent, the book from the reader.

During the same period, between 1876 and 1886, Henry Hobson Richardson (1838-1886), regarded as the most creative and influential architect of his time, designed six library buildings. The personal style that he developed became a national style which had an influence even in Europe. He used the alcove system in these libraries. They were designed for medium-sized communities, so the problem of shelving mass quantities of books was not an issue in design at that time, although it may have become so after the libraries were built. Richardson's main concern was to develop a highly individualized solution which, for the problem at hand, was actually quite functional. Richardson analyzed the functions of the library and its site and then developed a plan and elevations based upon his data. The plans were asymmetrical, responding to both function and site. Richardson's designs were severely criticized by Joseph J. Wheeler and Alfred Morton Githens in their book, *The American Public Library Building*, published in 1941. However, his buildings have held to the test of time and are being rediscovered today. They preserved the collections within them, served their public and are proving relatively easy to renovate and to enlarge.

Another major influence on American library architecture of the period was the librarian William Frederick Poole (1821-1894), who might be considered America's first library building consultant. His professional career spanned forty-seven years, paralleling the development of American librarianship during the nineteenth century. Poole began his great undertaking, an index to American periodicals, while an undergraduate, as the Assistant Librarian of the Brothers in Unity, one of two library societies at Yale University at that time. In 1851 he began his professional career, serving at the Boston Athenaeum and the Mercantile Library. He moved to the Boston Public Library when it opened in 1854, but returned to the Athenaeum in 1856 and remained there until 1868, when he resigned to become a "library agent," or consultant. Between 1869 and 1873 he served as a consultant for at least ten libraries, undertaking tasks that ranged from the preparation of book lists to the supervision of all the details in establishing a new library. At the same time, he became the librarian in Cincinnati and advised on the construction of that city's library, which was built from an unfinished structure originally intended to be an opera house.

Poole moved to Chicago in 1874, where, as librarian, he oversaw the construction of the Chicago Public Library. In 1887, he moved to the Newberry Library to develop another new library and its collections. The Newberry Library was the only building that Poole was able to plan from start to finish, and it was the crown of his career. In planning that building, he freed library design from the church-inspired architecture that reflected the library as a "temple of knowledge." In 1891, he wrote in the *Library*

Journal, "The same secular common-sense and the same adaptation of means to ends which have built the modern grain-elevator and reaper are needed for the reform of library architecture."[34] In the prairie city of Chicago, where ties to the past were freed and raw enthusiasm for new ideas flourished in the city's atmosphere and in its architecture, Poole was to set the tone for a new approach to library design using the new engineering techniques that were common to Chicago architecture, such as iron framing. He established standards for interior design that, while not specifically considered for the preservation of the collections, brought a new creative energy to the field.

The firm of McKim, Mead and White, established in the 1870s in New York City, was the most prestigious architectural firm at the turn of the century. Although it had introduced a new freedom of plan in residential design in the early 1880s, it turned to classicism as an expression of national architectural character, a concept that has caused considerable controversy in library design during this century. The firm designed a number of large libraries which were imitated by other architects. These included the Boston Public Library, the Low Memorial Library at Columbia University, and many of the branch libraries in the New York Public Library system. The firm also undertook alterations and a partial reconstruction after a fire of the University of Virginia Library, originally designed by Thomas Jefferson.

Boston Public Library, built in 1877, was designed in the classical style of the Italian Renaissance. The building was planned as a part of the urban design of Copley Square. From the beginning, it posed a series of functional problems. The architects spent much time designing and redesigning the various services inside the library as the library trustees kept changing the program. The architects used Labrouste's Bibliothèque Sainte-Geneviève as a model. However, they failed to make daring use of new materials or to carefully relate the books to the readers. The basic plan had a lobby in the front, with a grand interior staircase connecting to the second floor's great reading room that spanned the front of the building; the rear of the building held the bookstacks. In 1902, Robert Hoe, bibliophile and founder of the Grolier Club, using the pseudonym Henry French, offered his own criticism of library architecture modeled upon the Boston and New York Public Libraries: "Palatial fireproof buildings with imposing facades, monumental staircases and lofty halls and reading rooms, elaborate and learned classifications and systems of catalogues with ingenious machinery for almost automatic delivery of books to readers, however perfect and efficient, furnish no guarantees for the proper care of literary treasures."[35] Despite its physical drawbacks and the severe criticism that the Boston Public Library received from the day it opened, its basic plan was widely copied in most large public and academic libraries in America for the next fifty years.

In recent years, a revival of the Beaux-Arts tradition and the development of post-modern architecture has created new interest in the work of McKim, Mead and White. The firm's buildings contain certain functional problems, as do all buildings. However, an understanding and appreciation of the important qualities of a McKim, Mead and White building, or one influenced by the work of this firm, will help when dealing with its renovation. These buildings should not be dismissed as impossible; with imagination and a concern for the best of the architectural features they have to offer, they can be successfully renovated to house books and people. Today, the McKim, Mead and White Boston Public Library is viewed with appreciation by many, while its addition, completed in the 1960s, is now being criticized for its lack of function and disharmonious appearance.

Although a number of countries in Europe established national libraries in the seventeenth and eighteenth centuries, it was not until the early 1850s that the United States recognized its need for a national collection. It was not until the 1880s that a building to house the Library of Congress was planned; it was, and is today, the Library of Congress and not the national library. Bernard Richardson Green (1843-1914), a prominent civil and architectural engineer, was appointed Superintendent of Construction in 1888. Green previously had overseen the construction of the Washington Monument, the Army Medical Museum and Library, and the State War and Navy Department building, which housed the War Department's 45,000 volume library. He carefully analyzed the problems of shelving the 700,000 volumes in the library's collections at that time and the planned ultimate storage capacity of 4.4 million volumes.

Green's philosophy was that "a working library consists fundamentally of a collection of books and a number of readers, the object being to secure the most intimate practicable connection between them and at the same time preserve the books and their classification."[36] In speaking before the Washington, D.C., Library Association several years after the construction of the library, Green stated:

> When the building was begun eight years ago, bookstacks, properly so called, were few in number and small in extent, and probably the best existing example was that of Gore Hall extension at Harvard University. Its fundamental principles were excellent, and in its day ... it was a greatly advanced design . . . there was little to pattern after in designing the best possible stack—one which would provide the greatest security, convenience of access ... as well as the maximum storage capacity—and it was necessary to investigate the needs of the librarian, the readers, and the books themselves.[37]

Green followed the Ware-Winsor-Gore Hall system in the design for the War Department Library (1888), but it proved to have various shortcomings. The book stacks, similar to most manufactured between 1876 and 1897, the date of the construction of the Library of Congress, had a relatively crude finish, inconvenient or unreliable shelf adjustments, and primitive ventilation.[38] Green developed a list of eighteen "requisites" which paid particular attention to the care of books. He maintained that the ideal book stack should be free from fire, dust, weather, pests and vermin, not only through the stack area but also on each individual shelf.[39] Green's contribution to stack design included carefully made rust-free and easily adjustable shelves; effective communications and book conveying systems; adequate artificial light; and a ventilation system with sealed windows. His heavy reliance on artificial light and ventilation was another important contribution, particularly significant for the preservation of the library's materials. The Library of Congress building has had a profound influence on library design.

Green later wrote and lectured on ventilation and artificial light, noting reasons of economy for their use and their relationship to the preservation of books. He observed that "sunlight is often so bright and hot that it becomes injurious to the exposed books."[40] Most libraries built at the turn of the century had large windows to allow ample light for users. Too many libraries, oblivious to the harm that large windows cause to library collections, continue this tradition today.

In 1897, John Mervin Carriere (1858-1911) and Thomas Hastings (1860-1929) won the competition for the design of the New York Public Library, and the building was constructed between 1902 and 1911. The facade followed the classical model for libraries and museums. Its basic interior plan was conceived by Dr. John Shaw Billings, the director of the library. Billings served as mentor to the young Keyes Metcalf, who joined the staff in 1913, two years after the library opened. Billings' problem was to store millions of books and printed materials safely and securely with prompt delivery service. He devised a scheme to place the reading room at the back of the top floor, directly over the stacks, for access, following the Labrouste model at the Bibliothèque Sainte-Geneviève. Two inner courts provided light and air. Billings was concerned about the preservation of materials, and, for its day, the building was successful. There was a minimum of light in the stack area but a reasonable circulation of air. In the years that followed, New York Public Library was criticized for its Beaux Arts neo-classical style, which critics believed was incompatible with function. In reality, Billings' planning and Hastings' design were quite successful for the time. Today people are rediscovering the beauty of the building. As its interior restoration continues, the critics are learning that its space is not only beautiful but also functional, both as a public building symbolizing its prominent role in the cultural life of the city and also as one of the world's great research libraries. In the last decade of the nineteenth century, librarians were planning and architects were designing the new library buildings that were springing up in cities large and small around this country. Charles C. Soule (1842-1913), a trustee of the Brookline (Massachusetts) Public Library, who was neither a librarian nor an architect, was the first person to attempt to establish criteria for the planning and design of library buildings. At the American Library Association Conference in San Francisco in 1891, he presented twenty "Points of Agreement Among Librarians as to Library Architecture." These were reprinted in the conference issue of *Library Journal* in December 1891[41] and have had considerable impact on library planning and design. Nearly a century later several remain timely.

- A library building should be planned for library work.
- Every library building should be designed for the kind of work to be done, and the community to be served.
- The interior arrangement ought to be planned before the exterior is considered.
- No convenience of arrangement should ever be sacrificed for mere architectural effect.
- The plan should be adapted to probabilities and possibilities of growth and development.
- Simplicity of decoration is essential in the working rooms and the reading rooms.
- A library should be planned with a view to economical administration.
- The rooms for public use should be so arranged as to allow complete supervision with the fewest possible attendants.
- Modern library plans should provide accommodation for readers near the books they want to use, whatever system of shelving is adopted.

Although the care and preservation of the collections are not addressed specifically in the "Points of Agreement," they are inherent in them. Soule was quoted extensively by successive generations of librarians and architects, and each generation firmly believed that it was following his criteria. Yet each successive generation also believed that the previous generation neither followed nor understood them.

Perhaps the greatest impact on library design was caused by the industrialist Andrew Carnegie. As a young immigrant in Pennsylvania, he had made use of the library available to "working boys" in Allegheny City and vowed to establish free libraries should wealth befall him.[42] In 1890, Carnegie donated the funds to establish the Carnegie Free Library in Allegheny City. In 1897 he inaugurated the program which until 1916 provided the funds for the construction of 2,749 public library buildings and 116 academic library buildings throughout the country. Although these libraries were usually designed in the neo-classical style, the people involved in their planning consciously sought to design practical buildings. Despite Carnegie's concern for function, the new construction techniques and technologies that were being developed in the first half of the twentieth century quickly dated these buildings. The Carnegie libraries' eclectic style obscured any functional improvements in their design for the next generation. It is only within the past few years that their practicality is again being appreciated.

John Cotton Dana (1856-1929), librarian of the Newark (New Jersey) Free Public Library from 1901 to 1929, was an early advocate of an open library plan with free access to the collections. His niece Julia Sabine writes, "His letters and talks reinforced his intent to make the public library not only a treasure house of materials of the past, but a lively partner in any current educational activity, either formal or informal."[43] Dana was an early advocate of several important design concepts which did not become the norm until the 1940s, including easy access for the user, the open plan, and an aesthetic based upon the functional. Dana was at the forefront of the library profession with his concern for both function and aesthetics. The preservation of library materials, however, was not included in his vision.

Edward L. Tilton (1861-1933) was an architect who designed numerous libraries. He lectured and wrote extensively on library design during the first third of the century. Tilton was one of a group of library planners who pleaded for an emphasis on function, just as Justin Winsor had done a generation before and as Tilton's contemporary, John Cotton Dana, was doing. Tilton wrote an article on "Scientific Library Planning," published in *Library Journal* in 1912,[44] in which he stated that "proper library planning may now be called a science, since it is possible to formulate certain rules which, if carefully followed, will produce a methodical and rational result; it is likewise an art, since it calls for a skillful and systematic arrangement of means for the attainment of some desired end. The combination will produce a construction both practical and aesthetic."[45] Tilton listed specific formulas to calculate areas for each function, natural or artificial light, heating, ventilation and so on, based upon his investigations and his own library designs. In 1912, Tilton, working in concert with its librarian, Hiller C. Wellman, designed the Springfield (Massachusetts) Public Library. It was one of the earliest, if not the earliest, examples of what was later termed the "open plan." The main floor had a minimum of permanent partitions, a design which was advocated by Dana as early as 1900 but which did not become the norm until the 1940s. The open plan emphasized the importance of the first floor of the library building. Further, this plan acknowledged that natural light was neither necessary nor desirable in the book stacks, which were placed in the basement. Wheeler later brought this concept to its ultimate fruition in Baltimore's Enoch Pratt Free Library, which was built in 1933.

Alfred Dwight Foster Hamlin (1855-1926), who succeeded William Ware as director of the architectural program at Columbia University in 1903, was another advocate of library design that made services readily accessible to the reader. Angus Snead Macdonald, a leading figure in library planning and design during the first half of the century, was one of his students at

Columbia. In 1915, Hamlin contributed a chapter, "Some Essentials of Library Design," to the Snead and Company publication, Library Planning: Bookstacks and Shelving. Here he stated his thesis that "all libraries are a device for bringing books and readers together."[46] This seminal book on library planning and design for the twentieth century was prepared under the direction of Macdonald, who was then with his family firm which specialized in the manufacture of book stacks.

Angus Snead Macdonald (1883-1955) inherited his teacher's concern for access. His mother was the daughter of Charles Snead, the founder of Snead and Company, a manufacturer of architectural metal works. Macdonald determined on a career in architecture and studied at Columbia from 1901 to 1905. William Ware had been responsible for strengthening the concept of library book stacks in American libraries. By the time Macdonald enrolled at Columbia, the family company was a leading producer and supplier, having worked with Bernard Richardson Green to produce the stacks for the Library of Congress. Upon the completion of his degree in 1905, Macdonald joined the family company, which was then engaged in manufacturing the stacks for the New York Public Library. By 1915, Snead and Company had supplied stacks for over two hundred libraries in the country. Edward L. Tilton, who was involved in the planning of the New York Public Library when Macdonald joined the firm, used Snead stacks throughout his career. There was a long professional association between Snead and Company and Tilton, and later with Tilton's partner and successor, Alfred Morton Githens. Macdonald became president of the family firm in 1916. He continued to make improvements in stack design and became a pioneer in the development of a new theory of library planning and construction which led to the idea of a modular library, integrating the structural system, stacks, the reader and the mechanical system.

Macdonald first wrote about the modular library in an article, "The Library of the Future," originally published in Library Journal in 1933. The article had considerable

impact in the United States and abroad. Macdonald
continued to develop the theme of the modular library
until his death in 1955. Futurist Alvin Toffler has written,
"The contemporary library, Mr. Macdonald argued,
should throw out the cliches of monumentalism. It should
be built of light steel columns, beams and panels. The
columns should be hollow, providing vertical ducts for air
conditioning. The cool air should flow into hollow
chambers in the floors and be distributed into the rooms
through registers in the ceilings. The ceilings, themselves,
should be built to set off, not by load-bearing walls, but by
easily movable steel partitions. . . . Mr. Macdonald soon
became known in the library profession as 'Mr. Module,'
a tribute to his persistence and vigor."[47]

The concept of modular design was espoused by Alfred
Morton Githens (1896-1973) and Joseph J. Wheeler (1884-
1970) in their book, *The American Public Library Building: Its Planning and Design with Special Reference to
Administration and Service,* which was first published by
Scribners in 1941 and reissued by the American Library
Association in 1947. Although a number of texts, including Snead's, had already been written by architects and
librarians on planning and building libraries, this volume
was published at a critical moment. It ushered in a new
period of library planning and construction and served as
a text for the planning of library buildings for the next
twenty-three years. The book was the culmination of
Wheeler's years of experience and incorporated his ideas
about library buildings. Ironically, Wheeler's success was
based upon his planning for the Los Angeles Public
Library. The book was written with a tone of authority and
contained considerable data and drawings to convince
librarians that this was the way that libraries should be
designed. It carried forward the tradition of open, accessible libraries which had been advocated by Dana and
Tilton, and the modular concept first put forth by
Macdonald. Unfortunately, the authors' emphasis on
flexibility and accessiblity was achieved at the expense of
the library's physical environment. The lack of concern
for the storage and maintenance of collections came at a

time when the production of books was particularly poor and when, more than ever, books required an adequate environment if they were to survive even a decade in the library.

III. CONTEMPORARY LIBRARY DESIGN

The advent of World War II brought library construction to a halt. But even before the war was over, the country's leading academic librarians realized the impact that the returning soldiers, anxious to return to school and get on with their lives, would place upon their facilities. The Cooperative Committee on Library Building Plans was formed in 1944 by Harold W. Dodds, then president of Princeton University, to "concern itself with problems common to all of those interested in the planning of library buildings" and for the exchange of ideas.[48] Its membership included librarians from college and university libraries, with architects and engineers invited to participate in their meetings. Both Macdonald and Githens were included in the group, as were two librarians who were to make their mark as consultants in successive decades, Ralph E. Ellsworth and Keyes D. Metcalf. The committee met between 1944 and 1949 to review and discuss specific plans. Papers from three of these meetings were published (see the bibliography at the end of this section), including the report of the Orange Conference, held at Snead and Company's headquarters in Orange, Virginia, in October 1945. It was here that Macdonald unveiled his full-scale model of his modular library with its free-standing book stacks.

Macdonald's concepts attracted the attention of Ralph Ellsworth (1907-   ), who began planning the Iowa State University Library in 1943. Influenced by Macdonald, Ellsworth "wanted and got a plan totally different from anything previously built. He wanted flexibility to meet changing and unpredictable needs in higher education. . . . This first truly 'modular' building had a stunning impact on the library community."[49] In an article, "Educational Implications of the New Ideas in Library Construction," which appeared in *College and Research Libraries,* October 1946, Ellsworth wrote, "We are no longer content to confine our interest to 'collecting, preserving, and preparing for use' but we are now concerned with 'use' and all that goes with the term."[50] The preparation and preservation of collections were, quite literally, no longer as important as their acquisition and use. This approach to librarianship has had a devastating effect on library collections to the extent that materials which have been destroyed through neglect can no longer be used. A. Robert Rogers, in a survey article, "Library Buildings," published in the American Library Association's centennial volume, *A Century of Service* (1976), pointed out that "subsequent experience with modular building design indicated that use of hollow columns for ventilation ducts posed fire and other problems."[51] Ellsworth continued to advocate flexibility of structure to allow for expanding libraries and users and the accessibility of library materials in his books, articles, lectures and in his role as library consultant. He never expressed a concern for the library materials themselves.

Keyes DeWitt Metcalf (1889-1983) began his career at the age of fourteen as an assistant in the Oberlin College Library, where his brother-in-law, Azariah Root, was librarian. He later worked at the New York Public Library as it grew into a world-famous research institution, then served as librarian at Harvard University from 1937 to 1955. His career concluded with nearly thirty years of writing, speaking and consulting on library buildings in his "retirement." Metcalf witnessed the transformation of librarianship into a modern profession and the development of the library building from a facility to hold a collection of books to a complex institution using a variety of technologies to meet a variety of scholarly, informational, and recreational needs. He was a man of careful observation and consummate good sense. He welcomed the technical and structural developments that allowed for the better housing of materials and for better access by the public. But he never lost sight of the fact that the library's collections are its heart and that they must be cared for and housed properly so that the public could be well served. His years of observation and experience are reflected in his major contribution, *Planning Academic and Research Library Buildings,* published in 1966. Comprehensive in scope, this book immediately became the librarian's planning manual, no matter what the size or scope of the planned library, be it public, academic or research. Although no chapter is devoted exclusively to preservation, his concern for the physical care of collections is reflected throughout the volume. The material on the library environment, including heating, ventilation and lighting, remain timely today.

With Metcalf's blessing, Philip Leighton and David Weber of Stanford University, both experienced library planners and administrators, undertook a major revision of Metcalf's work that was published by the American Library Association in the fall of 1986. The changes in building technology in the twenty years since the first edition was published, and in our knowledge of materials, had been enormous. Further, although Metcalf was keenly aware of the impact of the new information technologies on library service and tried to advise his readers of their anticipated impact throughout his book, the technology could only have been imagined a quarter of a century before. Leighton and Weber were obliged to deal in a more concrete manner with the impact of these changes and innovations on library planning and design.

The result is less a definitive text than a philosophic statement of what academic libraries are. Leighton and Weber lead the library planner to reflection on how one might plan buildings to meet the needs of this, and the next, generation, in the age of information. They discuss the technology, the issues and the options and continue to remind their readers that there is no single correct way to plan a library building. Since 1966, the library and archival professions have learned that an ever-changing, ever-expanding technology can bring with it both benefits and disasters. A concern for the preservation of library and archival materials in all formats, from books and documents to online data bases, permeates this volume, for several building failures in the past decade have dramatically illustrated how vulnerable our collections are, and that without them we no longer have libraries and archives.

Ellsworth Mason (1917-   ) is another librarian and consultant who offers the voice of common sense as both a consultant and critic. Mason, a bookman with a doctorate in English literature from Yale University, served as the director of both the Hofstra and Colorado University Libraries, where he was an associate of Ellsworth. His writings on library buildings, including his cogent criticisms, have been assembled, annotated and reprinted in *Mason on Library Buildings*, published by Scarecrow Press in 1980. In the preface, he comments, "Over the past twenty years, in planning and consulting on more than a hundred and twenty buildings, I have seen the major forces that make for a good planning situation come together right only eight times."[52] This is a sobering statement. Mason's critiques of a number of mid-century buildings are a real contribution to the literature.

Although the consultants discussed here are known for their work in planning college and university libraries, they and other library consultants concerned themselves with the planning of public libraries in a post-Carnegie, post-World War II era. The concepts of accessibility and flexibility were particularly important in the planning of public libraries, which were to be welcoming community centers. Consultants such as Hoyt Galvin and Jerrold Orne in the United States; Margaret Beckman in Canada; Harry Faulkner Brown, Anthony Thompson and Godfrey Thompson in the United Kingdom; and Rolf Fuhlrott in West Germany, have written prolifically about public and academic library buildings. From the 1950s onward the American Library Association has held conferences on library planning on a regular basis and has published the proceedings, amply illustrated with plans. In the early 1960s *Library Journal* began publishing its annual architectural issue, filled with examples of "good" library planning and practical advice. Preservation, or more simply, the care and maintenance of the collections in the public library, was ignored.

A supermarket approach to library collections is reflected in the literature: appropriate siting in an accessible location, drive-in service, quick location of stock on open shelves, speedy check-out and little real concern for return of merchandise. Books were plentiful and reasonably inexpensive. The public library to some extent competed with the supermarket in making recreational reading available to a broad spectrum of readers. Special collections in public libraries were ignored; the library met the informational and recreational needs of the community at large. Until very recently, entertainment media and informational materials have been considered of limited, sort-term value; timely replacement rather than preservation was important.

Postwar library development in Europe was delayed by the need to rebuild damaged cities, but by the 1960s, European librarians were planning new buildings. New universities with post-modern libraries were springing up in Great Britain, Germany and France. The older universities were expanding their libraries and building new facilities to accommodate more students. For the first time, Western Europeans expressed a real interest in public libraries for the people. National libraries were expanded. British librarian Anthony Thompson noted, "A trend will be observed for the number of readers' seats to be increased sharply in the more recent buildings. This is a strange phenomenon, appearing at a time when national library networks are being developed in most countries, and one might expect a de-centralization of use, rather than a concentration at a national library."[53] Thompson further remarked, prophetically, "It seems that in the future each country may have to plan two national libraries, one for conservation and reference, and the other for lending and photocopying."[54] While American consultants toured the continent expounding theories of modular design, accessibility, flexibility and so on, European and Pacific Basin architects and librarians were also addressing these issues, with somewhat more concern for collections.

By the 1970s, funds were no longer available for collection development. As a result, librarians began to express concern for the physical condition of the materials already in their collections. In an issue of *Library Trends* (1972) devoted to library buildings, Harry Peterson wrote, "Libraries generally could benefit from a reexamination of their materials-handling systems, particularly with respect to acquisitions, processing and rebinding. In some cases there is need for improvement in the way books and other materials are obtained from and returned to the closed stacks."[55]

From its beginnings, the American Library Association has fostered a concern for the proper planning and construction of library buildings. It has encouraged debate and discussion, and during the past century it has published a considerable body of material on the topic. There have been a variety of committees that have compiled plans, prepared bibliographies and published debate. Since World War II, with the increased pressure to build and to expand, the committees have grown and merged into the Buildings and Equipment Section, Library Administration and Management Association (LAMA), with its own committee structure to foster the building and equipping of libraries for all constituencies. In recent years, this section has become more concerned with the problems of the preservation of collections. There is little question that the sensitivity of computer technology to the built environment has played a critical role in this awareness, but it has been accompanied by a concern for the more traditional materials. This section fostered the work of Leighton and Weber in the revision of Metcalf's book and sponsored the pre-conference, "Optimum Library Environment for Books and People," held in Los Angeles in 1983, which focused in a concrete way on planning and building structures that will protect collections. Today we can expect that the planning of libraries for collections and for people will go hand in hand.

The Preservation of Library Materials Section (PLMS) was formed in 1980 as part of the Resources and Technical Services Division (RTSD)* of the American Library Association. The members of this section have been vocal in raising the consciousness of librarians to the need for the proper housing, care and preservation of their collections. In 1981, Columbia University's School of Library Service established a sixth-year certificate program in Preservation Administration to provide advanced training in the preservation and conservation of library and archival materials. As more preservation specialists are trained with a knowledge of the physical nature of library and archival materials and their environmental requirements, they will play an increasingly important role as participants in an institution's planning team.

The Society of American Archivists (SAA) has an active Conservation Section whose members have been vocal and visible in the planning of archive repositories. The National Archives and Records Administration (NARA) is playing an important role by undertaking studies to document the most appropriate conditions for the long-term storage of a variety of media. *Preservation of Historical Records,* the joint report of the Committee on the Preservation of Historical Records, National Materials Advisory Board, and the Commission on Engineering and Technical Systems, National Research Council, presents some sound and practical guidelines for the storage and preservation of archival materials.

The National Information Standards Organization (NISO) Z39 Committee is in the process of developing standards for the housing and storage of library and archival materials. The museum community, national and international, encouraged by conservators and their professional organization, the International Institute for Conservation, are investigating and publishing more about the storage and preservation of art and artifact. Librarians and archivists have much to learn from the museum and conservation literature, as do curators and conservators from the library literature.

---

*RTSD is now the Association for Library Collections and Technical Services (ALCTS) of ALA.

Librarians and archivists, in the information age, have been obliged to be flexible in order to meet the ever-changing demands of new technologies and the users who demand information in a variety of formats and media. The library is no longer a warehouse of the past; it is poised on the threshold of the future. The body of information has expanded to a degree inconceivable to librarians and archivists a generation ago. Yet our role remains the same: to collect, organize, preserve, and make available the documents of our cultural heritage. The formats of our collections will dictate the design of the buildings that house them. The buildings that are planned in this decade must meet the demands of users until the end of the century and into the next. They must also provide a safe, secure home for the materials. As it was for their predecessors from the beginning of history, librarians and archivists need to plan repositories that are not only safe and sound, but flexible and accessible. There is no reason why these needs cannot be met with careful, knowledgeable planning, using the best that the current technology has to offer. The aesthetics of the building will continue to be debated; each generation will criticize the previous generation's design. But, in the main, library and archive buildings have worked reasonably well throughout history. Planners can learn from history, benefit from a knowledge of the mistakes of the past and attempt not to repeat them. Preservation and accessibility should and can work together.

NOTES

1. Hamden, CT: Archon Books, 1963, 15.
2. *Ibid.*, 21.
3. *A History of Writing.* London: The British Library, 1984, 14.
4. *Ibid.*, 17.
5. *Archives in the Ancient World.* Cambridge, MA: Harvard University Press, 1972, 3.
6. *Ibid.*, 54.
7. *Ibid.*, 58.
8. *Ibid.*, 77.
9. Gaur, 44.
10. Posner, 88.

11. Mohammed A. Hussein. *Origins of the Book*. Greenwich, CT: New York Graphic Society, 1972, 47.
12. Posner, 174.
13. *Ibid.*, 184-85.
14. *The Medieval Library*. New York: Hafner, 1963, 613.
15. "The Scriptorium," *The Medieval Library*, 605.
16. *The English Library Before 1700*. London: Athlone Press, 1958, 22.
17. Cambridge University Press, 1897, 62-63.
18. John Willis Clark. *The Care of Books*. Cambridge University Press, 1901, 143.
19. *Ibid.*, 132.
20. *Ibid.*, 171.
21. New York: New York University Press, 1972, ix.
22. Clark. *The Care of Books*, 232.
23. Banister Fletcher. *A History of Architecture*, 17th ed. New York: Scribner's, 1963, 659.
24. *Esthetique Monumentale*. Paris, 1902, transl. David T. Van Zanten, *Macmillan Encyclopedia of Architects*. New York: Free Press, 1982, 594.
25. Alvin Toffler. "Libraries," *Bricks and Mortarboard*. New York: Educational Facilities Laboratories, 1964, 73; reprinted in *Reader on the Library Building*, edit. Hal B. Schell. Englewood, CO: Microcard Editions Books, 1975, 32.
26. Van Zanten, 596.
27. John Morris. *The Library Disaster Preparedness Handbook*. Chicago: American Library Association, 1986, 34.
28. *Ibid.*
29. Charles H. Baumann. *The Influence of Angus Snead Macdonald and the Snead Bookstack on Library Architecture*. Metuchen, NJ: Scarecrow Press, 1972, 11.
30. *Ibid.*, 38.
31. Part I, 465-466.
32. Anthony Hobson. *Great Libraries*. New York: Putnam, 1970, 199.
33. Snead and Company Iron Works. *Library Planning; Bookstacks and Shelving*. Jersey City, NJ: 1915, 11.
34. Vol. 6, 70.
35. "Of Bibliophilism and the Proper Care of Literary Treasures," *Bibliographer*, Oct. 1902, 306.
36. "Planning and Construction of Library Buildings," *Library Journal*, vol. 25, Nov. 1900, 679.

37. Baumann, 69; from "Monuments of Books . . . ," *Washington Evening Star*, Nov. 27, 1896.
38. Baumann, 68.
39. Ibid., 69.
40. Snead & Company Iron Works, 118; reprinted from a paper read by Green at the Baltimore Meeting of the American Association for the Advancement of Science in 1909.
41. Vol. 6, 17-19.
42. Koch, Theodore W. *A Book of Carnegie Libraries*, New York: Wilson, 1917, 8.
43. *Encyclopedia of Library and Information Science*, vol. 6, New York: Marcel Dekker, 1971, 422.
44. Vol. 27, 497-501.
45. Ibid., 497.
46. 103.
47. Toffler/Schell, 33.
48. Cooperative Committee on Library Building Plans. *Planning the University Library Building*. Princeton, NJ: Princeton University Press, 1949, vii.
49. Walter C. Allen. "Library Buildings," *Library Trends*, vol. 25, July 1976, 102.
50. Vol. 7, no. 4, 327.
51. 234.
52. vii.
53. "Some Recent Trends in National Library Buildings," *Libri* 24:1, 1974, 75.
54. Ibid., 76.
55. "Developments in the Planning of Main Library Buildings," vol. 20, April 1972, 704.

BIBLIOGRAPHY

The bibliography that accompanies this section was selected to provide the reader with a survey of the history of library and archival planning and design from its beginnings to the present day. The readings represent neither the best nor the worst that has been written on library architecture. They reflect and report upon the state of the art as it has existed to the present. It is hoped that those who are planning a new building or the renovation of an older structure will find books and articles that will be helpful in conceptualizing an architectural project. Finally, it is hoped that a grasp of the history of the library as an institution and the facility that houses it will help planners, be they librarians, archivists, or architects, to produce a building that is pleasing to the people who will use it and protective of the materials that it contains.

The History of Library Design and Construction: General

Brichford, Maynard J. "A Brief History of the Physical Protection of Archives," *Conservation Administration News*, No. 31 (Oct. 1987), 10, 21.
   A brief history, with bibliography.

Bridenbaugh, Carl. *Peter Harrison: First American Architect.* Chapel Hill, NC: University of North Carolina Press, 1949. 195p. Illus.
   Biographical essay.

Cecchini, Giovanni. "Evoluzione Architettonico-Strutturale della Biblioteca Pubblic in Italia ˙dal Secolo XV al XVII," *Academie e Biblioteca d'Italia*, 35:1 (Jan.-Feb. 1967), 27-47. Illus.
   Describes the major libraries built between the 15th and the 17th centuries in Italy. Excellent bibliographic footnotes.

Clark, John Willis. *The Care of Books.* Cambridge: Cambridge Univ. Press, 1901. 330p. Reprint edition, Folcroft Press, 1973.
   History of libraries and of library planning and design.

Clark, John Willis. *Libraries in the Medieval and Renaissance Periods.* Chicago: Argonaut, 1968. 61p.
   A review of the characteristics of libraries and their development. The Rede Lecture, Cambridge University, 1894. Reprint of the 1894 ed.

Deitch, Joseph. "Portrait: Paul Goldberger," *Wilson Library Bulletin*, 61:5 (Jan. 1987), 54-57.
   An interview with an architectural critic with pithy comments on old and new American library buildings.

Dictionary of American Library Biography, ed. Bohdan S. Wynar. Littleton, CO: Libraries Unlimited, 1978. 596p.
Provides biographical information on American librarians.

Encyclopedia of Education, ed. Leo C. Deighton. New York: Macmillan, 1971.
Provides information on the history of libraries in the United States.

Fletcher, Banister. *A History of Architecture on the Comparative Method*. 17th ed., rev. by R.A. Cordingley. New York: Charles Scribner's Sons, 1963. 1,366p.
A classic text on architecture.

Gormley, Dennis M. "A Bibliographic Essay of Western Library Architecture to the Mid-Twentieth Century," *Journal of Library History*, 9:1 (Jan. 1974), 4-24.
Bibliographic article citing trends and the literature available on the history of library design. 78 citations.

Hobson, Anthony. "English Library Buildings of the 17th and 18th Century," *Offentliche und Private Bibliotheken im 17. und 18. Jahrhundert: Raritatenkammern Forschungsinstrumente oder Bildungsstatten?* Hrsg. Paul Raabe. Bremen u. Wolfenbuttel: Jacobi Verlag, 1977, 63-74. (Wolfenbutteler Forschungen, 2)
A summary of British library design. Hobson considers Wren's Trinity College Library, Cambridge, "one of the great glories of English architecture."

Hobson, Anthony. *Great Libraries*. New York: Putnam, 1970. 320p. Illus.
An illustrated history of selected libraries built from the Renaissance to the present.

Johnson, Elmer and Michael H. Harris. *History of Libraries in the Western World*, 3rd ed. rev. Metuchen, NJ: Scarecrow Press, 1976. 354p.
Brief history of how libraries developed and how they influenced or were influenced by their cultures. Bibliography.

Kaser, David. "Collection Building in American Universities," *University Library History*, ed. James Thompson. London: Bingley, 1980, 33-55.

Traces the development of American library collections over three and a half centuries. Covers Colonial period (1639-1780), 1780-1830, 1830-1880, the beginnings of teaching and research (1880-1930) and "service through cooperation" (1930-1980).

Lehmann, Edgar. *Die Bibliothekraume der Deutschen Kloster im Mittelalter*. Berlin: Akademie Verlag, 1957. 50 p. Illus. (Deutsche Akademie der Wissenschaften zu Berlin. Schriften zur Kunstgeschichte, 2)
A study of medieval monastic libraries in Germany.

Madan, Falconer. *Books in Manuscript*. London: Kegan, Paul, Trench, Truebner, 1893. 208p.
A basic study on early books, book production and libraries.

Marshall, D.N. *History of Libraries: Ancient and Medieval*. New Delhi: Oxford and IBH Publ.; Atlantic Highlands, NJ: Humanities Press, 1983. 151p.
A history with its strength in its coverage of Near and Far Eastern libraries.

Masson, Andre. *Le Decor des Bibliotheques du Moyen Age a la Revolution*. Geneva: Droz, 1972. 204p.
A history of the design and decoration of French libraries.

O'Gorman, James F. *The Architecture of the Monastic Library in Italy, 1300-1600*. New York: New York Univ. Press/College Art Association, 1972. 81p. and plates. Illus.
On the foundations of the library. Bibliography.

Pevsner, Nikolaus. *A History of Building Types*. London: Thames & Hudson, 1976. 352p.
Contains chapters on libraries and museums.

Pevsner, Nikolaus. "Libraries: Nutrimentum Spiritus," *Architectural Review*, 130:776 (Oct. 1961), 240-244.
A brief historical survey of architectural design.

Posner, Ernst. *Archives in the Ancient World*. Cambridge, MA: Harvard Univ. Press, 1972. 283p.
Describes the archival records and storage of the ancient world: Mesopotamia, Egypt, Greece, Persia, Ptolemaic and Roman Egypt, Rome, Parthian and Neo-Persian Empires. Inclusive bibliography and notes.

Richardson, Ernest Cushing. *The Beginnings of Libraries,* Hamden, CT: Archon Books, 1963. 176p. (Reprint of the Princeton, 1914 edition)
A discussion of the development of collections of information and communication in myth and in primitive society.

Streeter, Burnett Hillman. *The Chained Library; A Survey of Four Centuries in the Evolution of the English Library.* London: Macmillan, 1931. 368p.
The evolution of library design based upon the author's personal investigations.

Thompson, Donald E. "A History of Library Architecture: A Bibliographic Essay," *Journal of Library History,* 4:2 (April 1969), 133-141.
Covers general essays on libraries, ancient and medieval libraries, public and academic libraries.

Thompson, James, ed. *University Library History: An International Review.* London: Bingley, 1980. 330p.
A collection of essays with information on the development of university libraries.

Thompson, James Westfall. *Ancient Libraries.* Berkeley: University of California Press, 1940. 120p.
History of ancient libraries from their beginnings in the temples of Egypt and the fertile crescent through the fall of Rome (ca. 400 A.D.).

Thompson, James Westfall. *The Medieval Library.* New York, London: Hafner Publ. Co., 1965. 700 p. (Reprint of the 1939 edition)
A comprehensive intellectual history with contributions by specialists.

Wormold, Francis and C.E. Wright. *The English Library Before 1700.* London: Athlone Press, 1958. 273p.
Studies on the English medieval library; originally presented at the School of Librarianship and Archives, University College, London, 1952-54.

Library Design, 1850-1945

Allen, Walter C. "Library Buildings," Library Trends, 25:1 (July 1976), 89-112.
A historical review of library buildings and their design, 1876-1976. Author examines "a century of library architecture in relation to the changing perceptions of library functions, the development of building techniques and materials, fluctuating aesthetic fashions, and sometimes wildly erratic economic climates."

American Library Association. Library Buildings Round Table. "Proceedings of A.L.A. Conferences, 1936-1942." American Library Association Bulletin, vols. 30-36, 1936-42.
Summaries of the papers and discussion at each of these meetings.

Baumann, Charles H. The Influence of Angus Snead Macdonald and the Snead Bookstack on Library Architecture. Metuchen, NJ: Scarecrow Press, 1972. 307p.
An excellent history of Macdonald which encompasses the history of American library design.

Bentinck-Smith, William. Building a Great Library: The Coolidge Years at Harvard. Cambridge, MA: Harvard Univ. Press, 1976. 218p.
A history of the planning and building of the Weidener Library and the development of Harvard's library collections.

Bibliographical Planning Committee of Philadelphia. Philadelphia Libraries: A Survey of Facilities, Needs and Opportunities; A Report to the Carnegie Corporation of New York. Philadelphia: University of Pennsylvania Press, 1942. 95p.
An analysis of the library's postwar needs.

Bishop, William Warner. "The Historic Development of Library Buildings," Library Buildings for Library Service, ed. Herman Fussler. Chicago: American Library Association, 1947, pp. 1-11.
A review of European and American library buildings from the 19th century until World War II, written from an immediately postwar perspective.

Blake, Channing, "Carriere and Hastings," *Macmillan Encyclopedia of Architecture*. New York: Free Press, 1982, 387-388.

Bobinski, George S. *Carnegie Libraries*. Chicago: American Library Association, 1969. 257p.
A history of the Carnegie libraries and the contribution of Carnegie to American librarianship.

Bostwick, Arthur E. "The Librarian's Ideas of Library Design," *Architectural Forum*, 47:6 (Dec. 1927), 507-528.
Bostwick's statement of what a library should be: beautiful and utilitarian.

Byers, Edna Hanley. *College and University Library Buildings*, Chicago: American Library Association, 1939. 152p.
Contains photographs, floor plans, critical comment and other information about 42 buildings erected between 1917 and 1938.

Clayton, Howard, "The American College Library," *Journal of Library History*, 3:2 (April 1968), 120-137.
A survey of the beginnings of American higher education and the role of the library in its development.

Condit, Carl W. "The Building Arts in the Service of Librarianship," *Bulletin* of the Medical Library Association, 50:2 (April 1962), 167-176.
A historical overview of library building design; speech at the dedication of the opening of the National Library of Medicine, December 1961.

Dana, John C. "The Public and Its Public Library," *Popular Science Monthly*, 51 (June 1897), 242-253.
Dana's statement of what a public library is and should be, and how to accomplish it when planning the building. Preservation measures are confined to special and rare book materials.

Drury, Gertrude Gilbert. *The Library and Its Home*. New York: Wilson, 1933. 588p.
A collection of articles dealing with library construction.

Eastman, W.R. "Library Buildings," *Library Journal*, 26:8 (Aug. 1901), 38-43.

A program for the planning and construction of libraries at the end of the century, presented at the Waukesha (Wisc.) Conference. The lighting of libraries was emphasized; the preservation of the materials was not a factor to be considered.

Gerould, James Thayer. *The College Library Building: Its Planning and Equipment.* New York: Scribners, 1932. 116p.
A textbook on library planning with a common-sense approach for its day.

Githens, Alfred Morton, "The Architect and the Library Building," *Library Buildings for Library Service*, ed. Herman Fussler. Chicago: American Library Association, 1947, 94-106.
A statement about the buildings that the author, and others, designed and why they worked.

Githens, Alfred Morton. "Libraries," *Forms and Functions of Twentieth Century Architecture*, vol. 3, ed. Talbot Hamlin. New York: Columbia Univ. Press, 1952, 675-715. Illus.
A brief history of library design with the author's statement on functionalism. Githens outlines his recommendations for a good library plan; reviews types of libraries and their requirements.

Gormley, Dennis M. "A Bibliographic Essay of Western Library Architecture to the Mid-Twentieth Century," *Journal of Library History*, 9:1 (Jan. 1974), 4-24.
A bibliographic essay reviewing trends and the literature on the history of library design. 78 citations.

Green, Bernard R. "Planning and Construction of Library Buildings," *Library Journal*, 25:11 (Nov. 1900), 677-683.
The planner of the Library of Congress offers his views on library planning and design, with preservation and accessibility in mind. Green is critical of Poole's approach.

Greiff, Constance M., Mary W. Gibbons and Elizabeth G.C. Menzies. *Princeton Architecture: A Pictorial History of Town and Campus.* Princeton: Princeton Univ. Press, 1967. 200p. Illus.
American architectural history reflected in the community of Princeton, New Jersey.

Hadley, Chalmers. *Library Buildings, Notes and Plans.* Chicago: American Library Association, 1924. 154p.
  Emphasis on planning libraries for users and not as a piece of architecture. Stresses the importance of flexibility and expansion.

Harvard College Library. Dept. of Printing and Graphic Arts. *H.H. Richardson and His Office: A Centennial of His Move to Boston, 1874,* text by James F. O'Gorman. Cambridge, MA: Harvard University Library, 1974. 220p.
  Exhibition catalogue; selection of drawings.

Headicar, B.M. "Library Buildings of the Future," *The Library of the Future.* London: Allen and Unwin, 1936, 96-119.
  A description of the ideal library building, emphasizing comfort, convenience and the preservation of materials. Author acknowledges his debt to Macdonald and Githens.

Hermant, A. "Les Bibliotheques," *L'Architecture d'Aujourd'hui,* 9 (March 1938), 1-102. Illus.
  Issue devoted to the construction and equipment of libraries.

Higgenbotham, Barbara Buckner. *Our Past Preserved: A History of American Library Preservation, 1876-1910.* Boston, MA: G.K. Hall, 1990. 346p.
  Describes environmental concerns of librarians during this period.

Klauder, Charles Z. and Herbert C. Wise. "Libraries," *College Architecture in America.* New York: Scribner, 1929, 70-92.
  A statement on library planning and design based upon beauty and accessibility.

Larson, Jens Frederick. "The University Library," *Architectural Forum,* 54:6 (June 1931), 741-749.
  An article on the elements of a university library, offering guidelines for temperature, humidity and lighting.

McColvin, Lionel R., ed. *A Survey of Libraries, Report on a Survey Made by the Library Association during 1936-1937.* London: The Library Association, 1938. 719p.
  A survey of library buildings throughout the world.

Macdonald, Angus Snead. "A Library of the Future," *Library Journal*, 58: (Dec. 1 & 15, 1933) 971-975, 1023-1025.

Speculation on the changes in society caused by industrialization and the role that the library should play as the "people's university," for the productive use of leisure time. Macdonald discusses his ideal library to meet the need, noting the need for temperature and humidity controls for comfort and for the preservation of the books.

Macmillan Encyclopedia of Architecture. New York: Free Press, 1982. 5 vols.

A valuable source of information on architecture.

Mauran, John Lawrence. "The Relation of the Architect to the Librarian," *Library Journal*, 26:8 (August 1901), 43-46.

The article, in the Waukesha Conference issue, reflects a change of focus from "safeguarding the precious books themselves" to "the advanced theory of placing their precious contents within easy reach of all."

Munthe, Wilhelm. *American Librarianship from a European Angle; An Attempt at an Evaluation of Policies and Activities*. Chicago: American Library Association, 1939. 191p.

A review of the development of American librarianship, with a chapter on American library buildings.

Munthe, Wilhelm. "Modern American Library Buildings," *Library Association Record*, 3rd series, 2 (1932), 238-244, 283-290, 341-346, 371-379.

Report of a study tour to major American libraries; praises the ingenuity in planning buildings and solving problems.

Pashcenko, F.N. "Voprosy Stroitel'stva Knigo-Khranilisch," *Krasnyi Bibliotekari* (Moscow), No. 6 (1938), 52-57.

Discussion of problems of library buildings and of requirements of efficient library administration such as good lighting, prevention of fire hazards, correctness of book stacks.

Poole, William F. "The Construction of Library Buildings," *American Architect and Building News*, 10:299 (Sept. 17, 1881), 131-134.

A paper read at the Convention of Librarians, Washington, D.C., in which Poole refutes the "conventional" style of library design. He cites the Boston Public Library, with its wasted space, as an example. Mentions the problem of heating such buildings and the effect of the heat on the books.

Ranck, Samuel H. "The Library Building of the Future," *Library Journal*, 51:19 (Nov. 1, 1926), 959-961.
   Advocates the library as the intellectual center of a community rather than a repository for rare and precious objects.

Reed, Henry Hope. *The New York Public Library: Its Architecture and Decoration*. New York: Norton, 1986. 288p. Illus. (Classical America Series in Art and Architecture)
   A history of the library's planning and design. Glossary of architectural terms.

Reynolds, Helen Margaret. "University Library Buildings in the United States, 1890-1939," *College and Research Libraries*, 14:2 (April 1953), 149-156, 166.
   Covers "buildings designed for the library purposes of the university and housing exclusively or primarily the university's library materials."

Rogers, A. Robert. "Library Buildings," *A Century of Service*, ed. Sidney L. Jackson, Eleanor B. Herling and E.J. Josey. Chicago: American Library Association, 1976, 221-242.
   A history of American library buildings, with a discussion of practices that were destructive to books. Bibliography.

Sabine, Julia. "John Cotton Dana," *Encyclopedia of Library and Information Science*, vol. 6. New York: Dekker, 1971, 417-423.
   A biographical essay by Dana's niece.

Shores, Louis. *Origins of the American College Library: 1630-1800*. New York: Barnes and Noble, 1935. 290p. (George Peabody College for Teachers, Contributions to Education, 134)
   A history of the nine colonial college libraries.

Small, Herbert. *The Library of Congress; Its Architecture and Decoration*. New York: Norton, 1982. 215p. (Classical America Series)
   A guide to the architecture of the library; originally published in 1901.

Smith, R.S. "The History of Academic Library Buildings," *University Library History*, ed. James Thompson. London: Bingley, 1980, 128-146.
A brief, clearly written history of the development of university libraries.

Snead and Company Iron Works. *Library Planning, Bookstacks and Shelving: With Contributions from the Architects' and Librarians' Point of View*. Jersey City, NJ: Snead, 1915. 271p.
Case studies and comments from contemporaries in the field.

Soule, Charles C. "Boston Public Library," *Library Journal*, 17:2-4 (Feb.-April 1892), 54-55, 88-93, 124-125.
Soule's review of the library, criticizing the space and its "restrictive" effect.

Soule, Charles C. *How to Plan a Library Building for Library Work*. Boston: The Boston Book Company, 1912. 403p. (Useful Reference Series, 7)
Emphasis on utility, with information on construction.

Soule, Charles C. "Libraries," *Dictionary of Architecture*, vol. 2, ed. Russell Sturges. New York: Macmillan, 1901, col. 749-759.
A brief history of library design and current thinking, including eight of Soule's points of agreement. Soule presents what he believes should be the plan for a library.

Soule, Charles C. *Library Rooms and Buildings*. Boston: Houghton Mifflin, 1902. 24p. (American Library Association Publishing Board, Library Tract, 4)
An early work on library design and construction for circulating collections.

Soule, Charles C. "Points of Agreement Among Libraries as to Library Architecture," *Library Journal*, 16:12 (Dec. 1891), 17-19.
Advocates functional library design.

Stetson, Willis K. "Planning for Efficiency in Library Buildings," *Library Journal*, 36:9 (Sept. 1911), 467-468.
A plea for "economy," meaning flexibility and space in library design.

Thompson, Donald E. "Form vs. Function: Architecture and the College Library," Library Trends, 18:1 (July 1969), 37-47.
History of the development of the academic library, with a brief look toward the future.

Thompson, Donald E. "The History of Library Architecture: A Bibliographic Essay," Journal of Library History, 4:2 (April 1969), 133-141.
A bibliographical survey.

Thornton, John L. Special Library Methods: An Introduction to Special Librarianship. London: Grafton, 1940. 158p.
A text that reflects the low status of librarians in the pre-war period; notes that librarians had little or no say in library planning and design.

Tilton, Edward L. "Scientific Library Planning," Library Journal, 37:9 (Sept. 1912), 497-501.
Tilton produced formulas for the costs of constructing and equipping the library. The article was reprinted in the Snead and Company text in 1915.

Tilton, Edward L., Arthur E. Bostwick, and Samuel L. Ranck. "Essentials in Library Planning," Architectural Forum, 47:6 (Dec. 1927), 497-552; reprinted separately by the American Library Association in 1928.
Three articles and plans of libraries by the leading library architects and planners of the day.

Tombor, T. "Halado Ironyzatok Nagkonyvtarek Epitesenel," (Progressive Tendencies in Library Architecture), OMKDK Modsz Kiad., 37 (1971), 15-148.
Historical survey of library architecture and an analysis of the separate developments of European and American styles.

Van Rensselaer, Mariana Griswold. Henry Hobson Richardson and His Works, introd. William Morgan. New York: Dover, 1969. 152p.
A factual treatment of Richardson's life and work, issued two years after his death. Reprint of Houghton Mifflin, 1888 edition.

Van Zanten, David. "Henri Labrouste," Macmillan Encyclopedia of Architecture. New York: Free Press, 1982, 592-596.
A biographical profile of Labrouste and his work.

Warner, Frances and Charles H. Brown. "Some Fundamentals of College and University Library Buildings," *Library Journal,* 53:2 (Jan. 15, 1928), 85-87.
A lament on the poor planning of college and university library buildings and the lack of literature on the subject.

Wheeler, Joseph L. and Alfred M. Githens. *The American Public Library Building.* New York: Scribner, 1941. 484p.
The basic text for library planning and design in the post-war period.

Williamson, William Landram. "William Frederick Poole," *Encyclopedia of Library and Information Science,* vol. 23. New York: Dekker, 1978, 94-117.
Biographical essay on Poole.

Winsor, Justin. "Library Buildings," *Public Libraries in the United States: Their History, Condition and Management.* Washington, DC: Govt. Print. Off., 1896, 465-475.
Describes the plan of a library with a million volume capacity; advocates that books be kept in closed stacks and that the building have space for a bindery and repair unit.

Woodbine, H. "Essay on Modern Methods of Book Storage," *Library Association Record,* 12 (Sept. 15, 1910), 446-454.
Discusses the then common storage systems: alcove, stack, and a combination of both, with a survey of materials used and their appropriateness for the protection of books.

Yust, William F. "Follies in Library Planning," *Library Journal,* 51:18 (Oct. 15, 1926), 901-904.
A list of 21 mistakes in library planning; a reflection of the conflict between Beaux Arts and modern design.

Library Design: 1945 to the Present

American Institute of Architects. *The Library Building.* Chicago: American Library Association, 1947. 50p. (Building Type Reference Guide, No. 3)
Report based on the work of the American Library Association Special Committee on Post War Planning; reports "the most authoritative opinions on theories and trends in library

practice" to assist the librarian in planning to avoid "early functional obsolescence." Bibliography.

Architectural Record. "University Libraries; Architectural Record's Building Types Study No. 119," *Architectural Record*, 100:5 (Nov. 1946), 97-121.
A report on new developments in equipment, with case studies, based upon the survey by the Cooperative Committee on Library Buildings.

Barlow, S.H. "Library Buildings of the Future," *Library World*, 51:586 (April 1949), 195-197.
A proposal for a flexible, centrally located public library; no concern for the care of collections.

Bean, Donald E. and Ralph E. Ellsworth. *Modular Planning for College and Small University Libraries*. Iowa City, IA: Privately Printed by the Authors, 1948. 27p. Illus.
Planning and working with the architect; emphasis on modular construction.

Beckman, Margaret. "Colloque sur la Construction des Bibliothèques Nationales, Rome September 1973," *Canadian Library Journal*, 30:6 (Nov.-Dec. 1973), 475-480.
A report by the Canadian delegate on the IFLA conference on the planning of national libraries.

Brown, Harry Faulkner. "University Library Buildings: Library Planning," *Architectural Journal*, 147:8 (Feb 21, 1968), 457-460.
Discusses the flexible building which "provides a comfortable and efficient environment for books and readers." Notes the need for air conditioning for preservation, citing the *Report of the Committee on Libraries* (Parry Report) issued in 1967.

"Buildings and Equipment for Archives," *Bulletin of the National Archives*, No. 6 (June 1944), 149-180; 32p.
Papers presented at the Seventh Annual Meeting of the Society of American Archivists address many of the questions raised by the destruction of public records during the war. Discussion centered on buildings and equipment necessary for housing non-current records.

Burchard, John E. "Postwar Library Buildings," College and Research Libraries, 7:2 (April 1, 1946), 118-126.
  A report on the activity of the Cooperative Committee on Library Building Plans. Notes the need for planning and for new concepts of buildings and service to meet postwar demands.

Burchard, John E., Charles W. David and Julian P. Boyd. Planning the University Library Building; A Summary of Discussions by Librarians, Architects, and Engineers. Princeton, NJ: Princeton University Press, 1949. 141p. Plans.
  A report prepared by the Cooperative Committee on Library Building Plans at the beginning of the postwar period, as institutions of higher education were expanding to absorb the returning veterans seeking higher education. It focuses on flexibility, adaptability, expansion and growth in libraries, as well as ways of dealing with new technologies.

Collins, Will H. "Library Buildings After the War," Library Journal, 68 (Dec. 1, 1943), 1027-1030.
  A discussion of the planning for library buildings that took place during World War II.

Cooperative Committee on Library Building Plans. The North Carolina Conference. Philadelphia, PA: Stephenson Bros., 1947. 32p. Plans.
  Summary reports and critiques of buildings.

Cooperative Committee on Library Building Plans. The Orange Conference; A Meeting . . . Held at the Plant of Snead & Company, Orange, VA, Oct.26-28, 1945. Philadelphia, PA: Stephenson Bros., 1946. 88p.
  A conference addressing the requirements of library design in the postwar era. The need for air conditioning was stressed; lighting, security and fumigation problems were also discussed.

Cooperative Committee on Library Building Plans. The Second Conference. Philadelphia, PA: Stephenson Bros., 1947. 105p. Illus., plans.
  The committee met in a full-scale mock-up of the proposed new library at Princeton.

Davidson, Donald C. "Significant Developments in University Library Buildings," Library Trends, 18:2 (Oct. 1969), 125-137.

A discussion of the university libraries erected in the U.S. and in Great Britain in mid-century.

Ellsworth, Ralph E. "Educational Implications of the New Ideas in Library Construction," *College and Research Libraries*, 7:4 (Oct. 1946), 326-329.
    Advocates the modular, functional approach to library design, using new technology.

Ellsworth, Ralph E. "Library Architecture and Buildings," *Library Quarterly*, 25:1 (Jan. 1955), 66-75.
    Writes about the shift from Beaux Arts to functional design and notes new trends of service based upon subject arrangement, modular design, and making libraries more welcoming to the public. Discusses new materials, such as fluorescent lighting and air conditioning.

Ellsworth, Ralph E. *Planning Manual for Academic Library Buildings*. Metuchen, NJ: Scarecrow Press, 1973. 159p.
    Reviews a quarter century of modular design for libraries and concludes that it has been successful.

Ellsworth, Ralph E. *Planning the College and University Library Building: A Book for Campus Planners and Architects*. Boulder, CO: University of Colorado, 1960. 102p.; 2nd ed. Boulder, CO: Pruett, 1968. 145p.
    Discusses the modular layout, the divisional plan and the arrangements of various elements. Preservation is considered in the section on "Special Collection and Rare Book Rooms."

Ellsworth, Ralph E. "Some Observations on the Architectural Style, Size and Cost of Libraries," *Journal of Academic Librarianship*, 1:5 (Nov. 1975), 16-19.
    Discusses the stylistic and philosophical changes in modern academic libraries, raising questions of cost and collection development; no thought given to collection management.

Fussler, Herman, ed. *Library Buildings for Library Service*. Chicago: American Library Association, 1947. 216p. (University of Chicago Studies in Library Science)
    An introduction to postwar library design with its emphasis on function. Papers presented before the Library Institute at the University of Chicago, August 1946.

Githens, Alfred Morton. "Theory of Branch Library Design," *Library Journal*, 70 (July 1945), 609-613.
A survey of New York City's library buildings and the plans for the city's future needs. The emphasis is on efficiency, accessibility and publicity.

Hudnut, Joseph. "Architect and Librarian," *Library Quarterly*, 18:2 (April 1948), 93-99.
Thoughts on the relationship between architecture and libraries.

Humphreys, K.W., ed. *Colloquium on University Library Buildings*. Birmingham and Lausanne, 1972. 154p. (*Libri*, Suppl. 1)
Papers by building and technical consultants of international reputation, including Ellsworth and Metcalf. Proceedings of a seminar sponsored by the Buildings Committee and the University Libraries Sub-Section, International Federation of Library Associations (IFLA), Summer, 1967.

Isaev, E. "Sovremennye Trebovaniya k Planirovke i Oborudovaniyu Bibliothek," (Contemporary Problems in the Planning and Equipping of a Library), *Bibliotekar* (Moscow), 10 (Oct. 1970), 46-49.
Discusses the planning of municipal and regional libraries.

Kaser, David. "Twenty-Five Years of Academic Library Building Planning," *College and Research Libraries*, 45:4 (July 1984), 268-281.
Discusses the evolution of the modular design concept over the past 25 years and the problems that modifications to the basic concept have caused.

Kay, Jane Holtz. "Ideals and Axioms: Library Architecture." *American Libraries*, 5:5 (May 1974), 240-246.
Argues that libraries are designed for appearance rather than use and suggests that the purpose of the library and the requirements of the user should be the primary considerations in library planning.

Keally, Francis. "Planning the Modern Public Library," *The Bookmark*, 15:10 (July 1956), 231-236.
A general article reflecting the library concerns of the 1950s. Expresses a concern for the preservation of library materials through appropriate planning and construction.

Langmead, Stephen and Margaret Beckman. *New Library Design: Guidelines to Planning Academic Library Buildings.* Toronto: Wiley, 1970. 117p. Illus.

A study based upon the planning of the University of Guelph library. Emphasis is placed on accessibility.

Library Building Institute. *Problems in Planning Library Facilities: Consultants, Architects, Plans and Critiques.* Chicago: American Library Association, 1964. 208p. Illus.

Proceedings of an institute conducted in Chicago in July 1963. Participants included librarians, architects and library consultants. Plans for college and university, public, school and institutional libraries were presented and reviewed.

Macdonald, Angus Snead. "Building Design for Library Management," *Library Trends,* 2:3 (Jan. 1954), 463-469.

Stresses the management approach to "elasticity," or functional library design.

Macdonald, Angus Snead. "Looking Backward and Forward in Library Planning," *South African Libraries,* 21 (1953), 3-7.

Author states his philosophy of libraries in the postwar period.

Macdonald, Angus Snead. "Some Comments on Modular Libraries," *Proceedings of the Fifth and Sixth Library Building Plans Institute.* Chicago: Association of College and Research Libraries, 1955, 155-157. (ACRL Monograph, 15)

Describes how to use modular construction successfully.

McDonald, Joseph A. and Donald H. Hunt. *Public Library Architecture.* Philadelphia: Drexel Press, 1967. 99p. (Drexel Library School Series, 20)

Conference proceedings; a synthesis of the past 25 years.

Mason, Ellsworth. *Mason on Library Buildings.* Metuchen, NJ: Scarecrow Press, 1980. 331p.

A collection of Mason's articles and his reflections, looking back upon the past forty years of library design and construction.

Metcalf, Keyes DeWitt. *Planning Academic and Research Library Buildings.* New York: McGraw-Hill, 1965. 431p.

The comprehensive manual for the planning of all library buildings for the past twenty years.

Metcalf, Keyes DeWitt. *Random Recollections of an Ana-
chronism, or, Seventy-Five Years of Library Work.* New York:
Readex Books, 1980. 401p.
    Metcalf's autobiography, through his New York Public
Library years; an informal history of library planning in
America.

Panagiotou, Evalambia. "University Library Buildings: A View
from Greece," *New Library World*, 74:874 (April 1973), 81-82.
    Comparison of Greek, British and U.S. academic libraries.

Peterson, Harry N. "Developments in the Planning of Main
Library Buildings," *Library Trends*, 20:4 (April, 1972), 693-741.
    A discussion of planning for public libraries, based upon a
survey of large and medium-sized libraries.

Randall, William M. "Some Principles for Library Planning,"
College and Research Libraries, 7:4 (Oct. 1946), 319-325.
    Emphasis on functionalism, equated with beauty.

Reese, Ernest J. "Building Planning and Equipment," *Library
Trends*, 1:1 (July 1952), 136-155.
    A summary of postwar building trends: planning based on
reader's needs, modular construction, security, and environment for people.

Reynolds, J.D. *The Future of Library Buildings.* London: The
Library Association, London and Home Counties Branch, 1968.
36p.
    A feasibility study undertaken to help librarians and archi-
tects determine what a library is and to address the need for
planning and design.

Sanders, Harry, Jr. "Design Fashions and Fads in University
Libraries," *Library Trends*, 18:2 (Oct. 1969), 117-124.
    An excellent discussion of trends in design in which library
materials were rarely considered.

Schell, Hal B., ed. *Reader on Library Buildings.* Englewood, CO:
Microcard Editions, 1975. 359p.
    A compilation of articles by leading authorities on all aspects
of library planning.

"Standards for College Libraries," *College and Research Libraries News*, 36:5 (Oct. 1985), 277-279.
The primary concern of these American Library Association guidelines is design for use.

Thompson, Anthony. "Library Planning: Principles and Plan Types." *Architects' Journal*, 141:8 (Feb. 24, 1965), 493-500.
Outlines principles upon which library design should be based. Includes a brief historical survey of library building types.

Thompson, Anthony. "Some Recent Trends in National Library Buildings," *Libri*, 24:1 (1974), 69-77.
A summary of recent trends, following the Colloquium on National Library Buildings, Rome, 1973. Expresses concern that insufficient attention is paid to preservation/conservation.

Toffler, Alvin. "Libraries," *Reader on Library Buildings*, ed. Hal B. Schell. Englewood, CO: Microcard Editions, 1975, 30-49.
A futurist's look at the past and future of libraries. Reprint from *Bricks and Mortarboard*. New York: Educational Facilities Laboratories, 1964.

Weber, David C., ed. "University Library Buildings, *Library Trends*, 18:2 (Oct. 1969), 107-270; entire issue.
A collection of essays covering all aspects of university library planning.

PART TWO:

A GUIDE TO THE LITERATURE

CHAPTER 1. Planning: The Librarian, the Consultant, and the Architect

THE BUILDING IS THE FIRST line of defense in preserving library and archival collections. It is their home. A good home, sound and well built, will extend the life of the materials within and will also provide a good environment for the people who come to use the collection. If everyone involved with planning the facility remembers this, whether building a new repository or remodeling or renovating an older one, then a structure that is a suitable and proper place for people, books and other materials should be the outcome.

German librarian Robert K. Jopp has observed, "Library buildings should provide for the most appropriate conditions for the stay and for the activities of readers and librarians as well as for storing, treatment and use of books and other media."[1] This is a realistic and practical goal, but it calls for careful, detailed planning. The preservation of the collection is essential and should be a major consideration from the beginning of the planning process. The librarian or archivist, the staff, the architect, the consultant and, in many cases, a committee or board must work together to accomplish it. However, the functional success of a library building or archives repository is largely a result of the administrator's effort.

Library, archival, and architectural literature are replete with articles filled with advice for both the administrator and the architect; as long as libraries, archives, and other public buildings have been erected, there has been no lack of published advice on their construction and criticism of their outcome. A common misconception that appears in much of the current literature is that planning for people and planning adequate repositories for library materials somehow are not compatible. In recent years emphasis has been placed on the former, often to the detriment of the latter. Guy Sylvestre, the former National Librarian of Canada, has observed, "The new philosophy of librarianship, which has put the accent on communication rather than . . . on conservation, is unavoidably reflected in a new approach to library buildings. Accessibility is now the main consideration in the planning of new libraries."[2]

In reality, libraries built for people should also be appropriate for housing the materials for the people—books, computers, and a wide variety of other materials that make up the library/information center serving the community, institution, or corporation. "User-friendly," "accessible" libraries can provide an environment that reflects a concern for the materials that the users have come to use. We are learning that many users are uncomfortable when they sense that librarians and archivists are not taking proper care of the materials.

The articles listed in the bibliography for this chapter discuss the roles of the library or archival administrator, the staff, the architect, the consultant and the committees of trustees, faculty, or others involved in the planning of a library building. Some articles strongly recommend a planning committee, others recommend against one. In reality, most librarians, archivists, and architects will be obliged to work with some kind of planning committee, although observation and history illustrate that a committee's taste is nobody's taste. The role of the consultant can be a critical factor in producing a final design that is both pleasing and appropriate for the needs of the users, the staff, and for the materials that a repository is to house. Needs will differ dramatically from one community to the next, from one library or archive to another. Each repository has to be planned to meet the needs of its unique situation, based upon a sound understanding of design and construction.

THE LIBRARIAN

L.J. Anthony, in an article published in 1967, has written:

> The responsibility for providing a functional unit is the
> librarian's. He may work closely with management, archi-
> tects, and engineers, but in the last resort he is the only one
> who appreciates the purposes for which the accommoda-
> tion is designed and it is his job to ensure that the
> functional aspects are not subdivided to other require-
> ments.[3]

At some point in a professional career, nearly every
librarian or archivist will be involved in the building or
renovation of a facility. "Planning a new library building
is expensive and complicated. It is exhilarating and may
be one of the most pleasant, demanding, frustrating, and
satisfying activities that a librarian can undertake," write
Leighton and Weber in their revised edition of Keyes
Metcalf's *Planning Academic and Research Library
Buildings*.[4]

Librarians and archivists, with several notable excep-
tions, have not always been able to play an important role
in the design of their buildings. During the past century
many administrators have been dominated by committees, boards, donors, and/or architects. However, a careful
reading of the literature reveals that too often the administrator has been ignorant of the needs of the users, good
design, and most of all, a clear concept of library or
archival planning. Courses on planning library and archive buildings have never been an integral part of the
North American library school curriculum even though
most graduates will be involved in this process at some
point in their careers. Courses that instruct librarians on
how users *should* use the library/information center
abound. Library schools have taught their students to go
forth unto the world as purveyors of culture and information with little understanding of how culture and information are perceived by society at large. Only now are
actual user needs being considered and the librarian's role

as librarian and/or information scientist being reevaluated. First we need to know far more about who our clients are and how they perceive the library. Then we will be able to allow *their* needs, not our perception of their needs, to guide us in the planning of libraries that will collect, organize, preserve, and disseminate information in a variety of formats.

THE PROGRAM

The first step for the administrator and the staff is the preparation of a *program*, a detailed statement of the requirements that will enable each component of the library or archive to function effectively. Architect William E. Diamond writes, "The program, representing the results of early basic, critical decisions, is a statement of requirements for the facility to be built and is associated with a budget."[5] Angus Snead Macdonald, a trained architect and the intellectual precursor of today's library planners, observed toward the end of a career that spanned the first half of this century:

> The leading factor in getting a good library building is a clear-cut statement, in black and white, of the management's requirements. With such a program, the architect can be guided and controlled. Without it he is likely to take the bit in his teeth and produce a monument rather than a library. If that happens, the management must bear the principal responsibility, as the architect cannot be expected to meet needs of which he is not clearly informed. Preferably the architect and management will cooperate, each in command of his own field. Sometimes they will lock horns and compromises will be necessary; but if these are made wisely and after careful consideration, a good, well-balanced building is likely to result.[6]

Ralph Ellsworth, a librarian and building consultant, defines the program:

> Its main purpose is to give the architect a very clear, precise and detailed description of what librarians want their

building to do—its purposes and its operations. The secondary purposes are first, to force the librarian to think, which is hard for most of us librarians to do, but librarians must think through clearly and determine exactly what they want the building to be like. . . . A programme composed by a librarian should communicate in words. It is for the architect not the librarian to solve the problems architecturally. It is for the librarian to state problems in words and good words used properly.[7]

Rolf Myllar lists the essentials of a building program in a concise volume, *The Design of the Small Public Library*, which is a useful reference for the planning of any library building. He includes such basic information as a statement of the library philosophy including its history, objectives and policies, the building budget and any other information not covered by the library philosophy. He suggests that each space in the building be identified by name, type and number of occupants, required area in square feet, description of its specific function, its relationship to other areas, its special problems, a list of built-in equipment which becomes a part of the building construction cost, a list of movable furnishings which are under a separate budget from the building construction cost, a list of equipment required for the operation of the library (such as computer terminals) and a description of the atmosphere which the librarian may have in mind.[8]

The program will be changed many times before the building or renovation is completed, but if a carefully written plan is prepared, negotiation with the architect and a committee will be far easier and will greatly facilitate the role of the consultant. *The preparation of the program cannot be delegated.* It is the responsibility of the administrator with the assistance of his or her staff; if any member of the planning group shirks or delegates responsibility, the result will probably be an unfortunate building.

Once the "programming phase," as Ellsworth Mason terms it, is completed, the "design development phase" begins. It is at this point that the architect is selected and begins to work with the administrator and the planning committee. It is during this phase that the consultant, with the calm voice of reason, is most usefully employed to help the administrator, committee and staff cope with the three specters: the architect, growth and change.

THE CONSULTANT

There are a variety of library and archival building consultants available. The Library Administration and Management Association (LAMA) of the American Library Association (ALA) periodically issues a list of consultants from LAMA's membership; the list does not endorse anyone nor is it selective in any substantive way. The consultant may or may not be a professional librarian or archivist, although Ellsworth Mason, the dean of library consultants today, suggests that he or she be a member of our profession; there is no question that it helps. Keyes Metcalf suggested that the consultant have experience with three previous buildings; the "catch-22" is that someone has to hire the consultant to work on those first three buildings. A program which would allow the training of building consultants by having those interested work with a qualified consultant on three projects before branching out independently is very much needed by the library/archival community. The long and short of it is "caveat emptor"—buyer beware. However, by checking a consultant's previous work, noting how he or she was regarded by both client and architect, and by checking the amount of time he or she can devote to the project, one can make a reasoned choice.

Mason has observed that the consultant should be involved in the planning process from its inception, when his or her advice will have the greatest impact. The consultant will "focus a vague situation" and instill a confidence based on an experienced presence.[9] He or she will advise on the site and size of the library and will contribute to the creation of the actual building program. The consultant will also pinpoint sources of information and even assist in the search for architects and explain what is involved in working with them. The consultant's comments, as the design progresses, will frequently lead to a more functional and efficient building.[10]

Warren J. Haas of the Council on Library Resources has observed that "the role of the consultant changes with each assignment. The degree of involvement is governed by . . . needs and policy, and since they are bound to vary, it follows that there is no fixed relationship between [an institution] and its consultant."[11]

Keyes Metcalf puts it succinctly: "The mission of the consultant is to call to the attention of librarians and architects the problems they have to face, and to suggest different solutions to these problems rather than to tell them what to do."[12] The good building consultant will cast away the specters that haunt the administrator and his or her committee and facilitate communication with the architect during the design phase.

THE ARCHITECT

Metcalf writes, "Architectural style, aesthetics and interior decoration . . . are primarily the architect's responsibilities. He is the expert and, if problems arise on which he feels he should have help, he can call in an architectural or interior design consultant. He may in some cases have specialists in his organization for this work. Unless the architect has firm control over these matters, he can hardly provide a structure that has the desired unity."[13]

In Chapter 2, "Business, Art, and Profession of Architecture," in the fourth edition of *Building Design and Construction Handbook*, architect William E. Diamond writes, "The practice of architecture is a business, an art, and a profession. An architect, however, is primarily a professional. He is a qualified expert, licensed to practice. His functions are discharged primarily for the welfare of other than his own interest."[14] This article, and others in this bibliography, discuss the matter of contract and fee.

Myllar suggests two ways in which an architect should be chosen. The administrator and the committee (1) "may obtain someone whose work it knows and admires," or (2) "may invite several architects to be interviewed, ask them to bring examples of their work, and discuss with them their qualifications." Hiring an architect through a patronage system or because he or she will reduce the fee is not recommended.[15]

Today good architects are aware of environmental considerations in contemporary building design; many have had some experience with historic preservation or renovation. They should know a great deal about designing buildings for people, but they cannot be expected to know about designing buildings for library and archival materials, which come in a variety of media and formats. It is the responsibility of the administrator to advise the architect when popular design features such as underground construction, skylights, sunken gardens, and large windowed areas can cause harm to the materials. As this book is being written, library buildings and archive repositories are still being constructed or remodeled with harmful features such as these, and they continue to win awards for design.

In an article, "What Architects Need to Know, and Don't Want to Hear," specifically concerned with the design of museums, architect John D. Hilberry writes:

> Every architect *wants* to hear that he has been asked to give free reign to his creative talents by designing a building with few functional problems, a generous budget and a collection of art or artifacts to decorate his creation. On the other hand, what architects *need* to know is that they are confronted with a design problem as complex as a hospital, that the budget will be quickly consumed by difficult technical requirements and that while the building must achieve the highest level of design excellence and stand as a fine example of public architecture, it must be designed through a long and ambiguous process involving people who represent divergent and sometimes conflicting points of view and cannot always clearly define the program for the building.[16]

The message in this article is just as applicable to libraries and archives and the materials they house. It should serve as a reminder to the administrator and the planning committee of the complexity of their responsibility.

NOTES

1. Typescript of a paper presented at the 49th General Conference of the International Federation of Library Associations, Munich, 1983, 1.
2. Quoted in *New Library Design*, by Stephen Langmead and Margaret Beckman. Toronto: Wiley, 1970, v.
3. *Handbook of Special Librarianship and Information Work*, 3rd ed., London: Aslib, 1967, 310.
4. Chicago: American Library Association, 1986, 48.
5. "Business, Art and Profession of Architecture," *Building Design and Construction Handbook*, 4th ed., 27.
6. "Building Design for Library Management," *Library Trends*, 2:3 (1954), 469.
7. "Writing the Programme," *Planning the Academic Library*. Newcastle, Eng.: Oriel Press, 1971, 42.
8. NY: Bowker, 1966, 23.
9. "Managing the Planning of Library Buildings," *Current Concerns in Library Management*. Littleton, CO: Libraries Unlimited, 1979, 81.
10. Rolf Myllar, *The Design of the Small Public Library*. NY: Bowker, 1966, 11.
11. "The Role of the Building Consultant," *College and Research Libraries*, 40:3 (July 1969), 365.
12. "Concerning Future Planning Developments," *Planning the Academic Library*. Newcastle, Eng.: Oriel Press, 1971, 13.
13. *Planning Academic and Research Library Buildings*. NY: McGraw-Hill, 1965, 175.
14. NY: McGraw-Hill, 1982, 2-1.
15. Myllar, 25.
16. *Museum News*, 61:5 (June 1953), p.55.

BIBLIOGRAPHY

Planning: General Readings

Association for Recorded Sound Collections. Associated Audio Archives Committee. *Audio Preservation: A Planning Study*, ed. Elwood A. McKee. Rockville, MD: ARSC, 1987. 860p.

The final report of a study of the needs of archives for sound recordings. It is comprehensive in scope, with an extensive bibliography, including "A Bibliography of Materials on the Planning and Construction of Library Buildings," by Linda W. Blair, pp. 201-237. Essential for institutions with sound archives.

Banz, George. "Libraries," *Canadian Architect*, 7 (Feb. 1962), 42-44.
Practical advice on planning libraries, with the preservation of materials and a concern for the user presented so that they are compatible.*

Beckerman, Edwin P. "Planning and Construction of Buildings," *Local Public Library Administration*, 2nd rev. ed., Ellen Altman, ed. Chicago: American Library Association, 1980, 213-224.
A general summary article with a common-sense approach; emphasis on public services. Good discussion on the problems of the renovation of buildings for libraries.

Beckman, Margaret. "Library Buildings in the Network Environment," *Journal of Academic Librarianship*, 9:5 (Nov. 1983), 281-284.
Discussion about the impact that technology will have upon library buildings: installation, systems and operations. The author urges flexibility in planning a building.*

Boss, Richard W. *Information Technologies and Space Planning for Libraries and Information Centers*. Boston: G.K. Hall, 1987. 121p.
Describes the technologies that have the greatest impact on libraries and discusses their potential impact on facilities planning. Clearly and concisely written, with practical information. Preservation of materials and information is emphasized and advice on environmental requirements is given.*

Brown, Harry Faulkner, "The Initial Brief for an Academic Library and its Development," *Colloquium on University Library Buildings*. Birmingham, Eng. and Lausanne, Switz.: Libri, 1972, 13-27. (*Libri*, Bull. Suppl. 1)
Guidelines for preparing the program, with a list of 15 "quality and design factors," including environmental factors. Brief, basic.

Brown, Harry Faulkner. *Planning the Academic Library; Metcalf and Ellsworth at York*. Newcastle, Eng.: Oriel Press, 1971, 97p.

Useful discussion on planning; Metcalf is particularly concerned with the preservation of library collections. Papers and remarks by Keyes D. Metcalf and Ralph E. Ellsworth at a course on academic library planning held at the York Institute of Advanced Architectural Studies, 1966.

Brown, Henry Faulkner, "University Library Buildings: Library Planning," *Architects' Journal*, 147:8 (Feb. 21, 1968), 457-460.

Discusses the flexible building which "provides a comfortable and efficient environment for books and readers."

"Building Together," *Library Association Record*, 65:12 (Dec. 1963), 440-452.

Two papers, one by D.W. Dickenson, an architect, and the other by E.M. Broome, a librarian, in which they discuss the teamwork that is necessary for a successful library building.

Campbell, E.G. "Buildings and Records Equipment of Federal Records in the United States," *Archivum: Revue International des Archive*, 7 (1957), 21-25.

Guidelines for the design of record storage centers that are economical but safe for storage. Stresses safety from fire as well as shelving.

Carolin, Peter and M.J. Long. "AD Briefing: Libraries," *Architectural Design*, 44:7 (1974), 418-425.

Describes the elements for library areas, with recognition of the need for design to protect and preserve library materials.

Christian, John F. and Shonnie Finnegan. "On Planning an Archive," *American Archivist*, 37:4 (Oct. 1974), 573-578.

A helpful article on planning an archive with a checklist of building needs.

Cohen, Aaron and Elaine. *Behavioral Space Planning and Practical Design for Libraries*. Croton-on-Hudson, NY: The Authors, 1968. Unpaged notebook.

Workbook prepared for a seminar given by the authors, which contains useful information about design that can be applied when planning for preservation.

Cohen, Elaine and Aaron. "Do Our Library Buildings Have To Be Discarded Every Fifteen Years?" Library Journal Special Report, 1, 1976, 56-60.

A brief article on planning and caring for libraries, with a note that courses on library building design should be offered in library schools.

Cowgill, Clinton H. and George E. Pettengill. The Library Building. Washington, DC: American Institute of Architects, 1959. 32p. (AIA Building Type Reference Guide BTRG 3-3, 3-4)

A guide for the architect, student, and librarian. Covers planning, as well as heating, ventilation, air conditioning and lighting. Annotated bibliography. Reprinted from the American Institute of Architects Journal, May-June 1959.

Dahlgren, Anders C. "An Alternative to Library Building Standards," Illinois Libraries, 67:9 (Nov. 1985), 772-777.

Questions the use of rigidly drawn standards for library buildings; advocates "detailed local planning to address a specific local need."

Dahlgren, Anders C. Planning the Small Public Library Building. Chicago: American Library Association, 1985. 23p. (Small Libraries Publ., 11)

A pamphlet to give library planners from smaller communities a brief overview of the planning process.

Dahlgren, Anders C. and Erla P. Heyns, comp. Planning Library Buildings; A Select Bibliography. Chicago: Library Administration and Management Association, American Library Association, 1990. 60p.

Citations on planning and design that are appropriate for all types of libraries. No annotations.

Dewe, Michael, ed. Adaptation of Buildings To Library Use. New York, Munich: Saur, 1987. 254p. (IFLA Publication, 39)

An overview from an international perspective. Proceedings of a seminar held in Budapest, Hungary, June 1985.

Duchein, Michel. Archives Buildings and Equipment. Munich: Verlag Dokumentation, 1977. 201p. (ICA Handbook Series, 1)

Covers all aspects of construction and renovation with concern for the preservation of archival materials. Some additional material supplements the original edition. A translation of Les Batiments et Equipements d'Archives (Paris 1966), sponsored by the International Council on Archives.*

Eatough, Clair L. "What Tomorrow's Library Will Look Like," *Nation's Schools*, 77:3 (March 1966), 107-109.

A description of the Knowledge Resource Center of the future in America's schools.

Educational Facilities Laboratories. *The Impact of Technology on the Library Building*. New York: Educational Facilities Laboratories, July 1967. 20p.

A position paper covering computers, microforms, communications and implications for buildings, prepared by a panel of librarians, information specialists, social scientists and architects. Advocates building for expansion, dealing with both technology and the user. The physical environment of the library is mentioned throughout the report; a useful background document.

Edwards, Heather M. *University Library Building Planning*. Metuchen, NJ: Scarecrow Press, 1990. 145p. Illus.

Case studies of successful library buildings in the U.S., the U.K., and South Africa. Discusses recent library developments that may influence planning and gives practical advice on space, power, environment, security, and human considerations.

Ellsworth, Ralph E. "The ABCs of Remodeling/Enlarging an Academic Library Building: A Personal Statement," *Journal of Academic Librarianship*, 7:6 (Jan. 1982), 334-343.

Discusses when renovation is possible and how to work with the architect and consultant.

Ellsworth, Ralph E. *Academic Library Buildings: A Guide to Architectural Issues and Solutions*. Boulder, CO: Colorado Associated University Press, 1973. 530p. Illus.

A "working guide to the physical decisions made by planners in the resolution of issues peculiar to libraries." Concerned with flexibility and design for users, with little concern for the preservation of library materials. Some interiors shown are harmful for books and uncomfortable for people.

Ellsworth, Ralph E. *Planning the College and University Library Building: A Book for Campus Planners and Architects*. 2nd ed. Boulder, CO: Pruett Press, 1968. 145p. Illus.

Discusses the modular lay-out, divisional plan, and the arrangement of various elements. Preservation considerations are mentioned in the section on "Special Collections and Rare Book Rooms."

Feilden, Bernard M. and Giovanni Scichilone. "Museums: The Right Places for Conservation?" *Museum*, 34:1 (1982), 10-20.

An article on planning museums to protect their contents; security, environment and planning for exhibitions are covered. Much of this information can be applied to the planning of libraries and archives.

Flynn, John E. and Arthur W. Segil. *Architectural Interior Systems: Lighting, Air Conditioning, Acoustics.* New York: Van Nostrand Reinhold, 1970. 306p. (Van Nostrand Reinhold Environmental Engineering Series)

Written for architects with emphasis on "aspects of building design that affect human sensory response and behavior." A clearly written text, with diagrams.

Fuhlrott, Rolf. "Underground Libraries," *College and Research Libraries*, 47:3 (May 1986), 238-262. Illus.

A review of the 22 underground libraries constructed at time of writing. Bibliography.

Galvin, Hoyt R. and Martin Van Buren. *The Small Public Library.* Paris: UNESCO, 1959. 133p. (UNESCO Public Library Manuals, 10)

On planning the small library; discusses environment, including the effect of temperature, humidity and ventilation on books.

Gondos, Victor, Jr. "Archival Buildings—Programing and Planning," *Reader for Archives and Records Centers.* Chicago: Society of American Archivists, 1970, 3-19.

A clearly written statement of what is required to plan an archive or records storage center in which preservation of the material is recognized as a primary concern. Reprinted from *American Archivist*, 28:4 (October 1964).

HBW Associates, Inc. "Planning Aids for a New Library Building," *Illinois Libraries*, 67:9 (Nov. 1985), 794-810.

A series of planning aids to help the librarian understand the elements of a building program. Covers preliminary planning and interior materials, such as flooring, lighting, shelving and furnishings, that allow efficient maintenance. Bibliography.

Hall, Richard B. "The Library Space Utilization Methodology," *Library Journal*, 103:21 (Dec. 1, 1978), 2379-2383.

Presents in graphic form information about the functional

requirements of a library; an attempt to design a tool to facilitate the planning process and lead to more effective facilities.

The Handbook of Property Conservation, 2nd ed. Norwood, MA: Factory Mutual System, 1978. 240p.
Valuable information about planning; from the insurer's perspective.

Harvard University. Graduate School of Education. *Library Technology and Architecture*. Cambridge: Graduate School of Education, Harvard University, 1968. 51p.
Report of a conference held in 1967 "to investigate the implications of new technology for library architecture and to incorporate the findings into the planning for a new library/research facility" for Harvard's Graduate School of Education. The report deals with the impact of new technology upon the traditional view of a library.

Holt, Raymond M. *Planning Library Buildings and Facilities: From Concept to Completion* (The Library Administration Series, 9). Metuchen, NJ: Scarecrow Press, 1989. 260p. Illus.
Designed to assist administrators faced with the problems associated with designing a new or remodelled library building.

Irvine, Betty Jo. *Slide Libraries; A Guide for Academic Institutions and Museums*, 2nd ed. Littleton, CO: Libraries Unlimited, 1979. 321p.
A text on the design and management of slide libraries with a chapter on the necessary environmental controls. Bibliography on the care and preservation of films and slides.

Kaser, David. "Current Issues in Building Planning," *College and Research Libraries*, 50:3 (May 1989), 297-304.
As librarians prepare to replace or remodel older structures, they need to determine the information needs of future users, then plan facilities that can expand to meet them. A survey of needs is emphasized; program requirements are outlined.*

Kaser, David. "The Role of the Building in the Delivery of Library Service," *Access to Scholarly Information: Issues and Strategies*, Sul H. Lee, ed. Ann Arbor, MI: Pierian Press, 1985, 13-24.
While its emphasis is on planning a building for service, the chapter notes the harmful effect on library materials of light, poor air circulation and improperly maintained tem-

perature and humidity. It is brief, practical and clearly written.

Kay, Jane Holz. "Ideals and Axioms: Library Architecture," *American Libraries*, 5:5 (May 1974), 240-246.
   A plea for more common sense in library design, using what is best, not what is new. The author observes that standards can be carried to absurdity by unthinking planners.

Konya, Allen. *Libraries: A Briefing and Design Guide*. London: Architectural Press; New York: Van Nostrand Reinhold, 1986. 182p. Illus.
   Section I provides basic advice on planning a building. Section II specifically deals with the planning of libraries. While storage and preservation of materials are not emphasized, standards are acknowledged in the text. Useful appendices and bibliography with British emphasis.

Lee, Sang Chul. *Planning and Design of Academic Library Buildings*. New York: School of Library Service, Columbia University, 1985. 449p. PhD. Diss.
   An investigation of the perceptions of library directors, consultants and architects on issues relating to the planning and design of library buildings. Lengthy discussion on stack areas, heating, ventilation, light. Demonstrates the need for dialogue between librarians and architects.

Library Journal. *Library Space Planning*, ed. Karl Nyren. New York: 1976. 80p. (LJ Special Report, I)
   Issue covers energy, cooperation, library organization, new technology, collection development, site remodeling, community use.

Lieberfeld, Lawrence. "The Curious Case of the Library Building," *College and Research Libraries*, 44:4 (July 1983), 277-282.
   An argument against the use of formulas in library planning; urges libraries "to develop library building programs on the basis of its own needs without any predetermination or artificial assumptions hovering over the process."

Mason, Ellsworth. "Back to the Cave; or, Some Buildings I Have Known," *Library Journal*, 94:21 (Dec. 1, 1969), 4353-4357.
   Architectural planning of libraries is discussed with exam-

ples of mistakes that were made in specific libraries. Offers suggestions on how to avoid them in the future.

Mason, Ellsworth. "Managing the Planning of Library Buildings," Current Concepts in Library Management, Martha Boaz, ed. Littleton, CO: Libraries Unlimited, 1979, 180-190.
An excellent article on the planning process and the role of the librarian, the consultant and the architect. Sound advice on heating and air conditioning, lighting and plumbing.*

Mason, Ellsworth. Mason on Library Buildings. Metuchen, NJ: Scarecrow Press, 1980. 333p.
This volume of Mason's reflections and collected works provides a firm foundation for sound library planning. See especially Chapter 2, "Writing the Library Building Program," pp. 12-24, which originally appeared as "Some Advice to Librarians on Writing a Building Program," Library Journal, 91:21 (Dec. 1966).*

Merritt, Frederick S., ed. Building Design and Construction Handbook, 4th ed. New York: McGraw-Hill, 1982. 1479p.
A compendium of the best of current building design and construction practices; emphasis on fundamental principles and the potential applications of them. Originally published as the Building Construction Handbook.

Metcalf, Keyes D. Planning Academic and Research Library Buildings, 2nd ed. by Philip D. Leighton and David C. Weber. Chicago: American Library Association, 1986. 630p.
A philosophic approach to the planning of library buildings; takes into consideration the rapid developments in building technology and automation in libraries. The book is concerned with a safe and comfortable environment for materials and people.*

Metcalf, Keyes D. Planning Academic and Research Library Buildings. New York: McGraw-Hill, 1965. 431p.
The basic text for library planning and design for twenty years; the volume reflects the author's fifty years of experience in library planning and his concern for the library's collections.

Mount, Ellis, ed. Creative Planning of Special Library Facilities. New York: Haworth Press, 1988. 197p.

A basic text concerned with the planning and design of small library facilities.

Myllar, Rolf. *The Design of the Small Public Library*. New York: Bowker, 1966. 95p.

A concise, clearly written statement on library planning that can be applied to any library. Little specific reference to preservation, but its practical approach to problems of planning lends itself to planning for the preservation of materials as well as for libraries pleasing to people. Illustrated; bibliography.*

Novak, Gloria J. "Building Planning Austerity," *Austerity Management in Academic Libraries*, John F. Harvey and Peter Spyers-Duran, eds. Metuchen, NJ: Scarecrow Press, 1984, 185-204.

Author observes that austerity can lead to planning that will minimize waste and optimize investment. While the preservation of the collections is not a theme, information about planning for the building, HVAC and lighting systems is helpful.

Orr, J.M. *Designing Library Buildings for Activity*. London: Deutsch, 1972. 152p.

Written as a basic textbook for library design; a concern for the preservation of collections is reflected throughout the text.

Raikes, Deborah A. "Microform Storage in Libraries," *Library Technology Reports*, 12:3 (July-Aug. 1979), 445-448; "Survey," 449-558.

A summary of storage requirements followed by an analysis of equipment available on the market at time of publication.

Reece, Ernest J. "Library Building Programs: How to Draft Them," *College and Research Libraries*, 3:3 (July 1952), 198-211.

Assumes that the librarian and architect can work together toward a common goal. Stresses clear writing, free of jargon. Provides sound advice on the library planning process. Brief bibliography.

Rohlf, Robert H. "Essential Decisions Needed in Planning for the Remodelling of Libraries," *Catholic Library World*, 51:7 (Feb. 1980), 280-282.

A good discussion of the factors to be considered when deciding whether to renovate an older building or to construct a new one. Covers structure, electrical condition, mechanical systems and plumbing considerations.

Sannwald, William W. and Robert S. Smith. *Checklist of Library Building Design Considerations*. Chicago: American Library Association, 1988. 77p.
A list of questions to ask during the design phase of a new or remodelled library project.

Schell, Hal B., ed. *Reader on the Library Building*. Englewood, CO: Microcard Editions, 1975, 359p.
A collection of essays reprinted from other sources that cover various aspects of planning, designed to be used by those involved in the planning process.*

Smith, Beryl K., ed. *Space Planning for the Art Library*. Tucson, AZ: Art Libraries Society of North America, 1991. 32p. (Occasional Paper, 9)
Papers on the contribution of librarians, consultants and architects to building design. Papers given at the ARLIS/NA Annual Conference, Dallas, TX 1988.

Smith, Richard D. "Fumigation Dilemma: More Overkill or Common Sense," *The New Library Scene*, 3:6 (Dec. 1984), 1,5-6.
A discussion of the problem of fumigation in the light of current Occupational Safety and Health Administration (OSHA) standards for the use of ethylene oxide. Because of the problems of chemical fumigation, this article should be read as construction is being planned.

Snyder, Richard L. *College Library Buildings in Transition—Looking at the 1980s*. ERIC Clearinghouse, 1984. 44p. Typescript.
Discusses the effects of technological developments on the planning of libraries. Covers design and construction considerations, heating and air conditioning, lighting, heating safety and security. Emphasis on flexibility. Based on a talk given at the Conference on College and Academic Library Buildings in the '80's, New Stanton, PA, 1983.

Spreitzer, Francis F. "Library Microform Facilities," *Library Technology Reports*, 12:4 (July 1976), 407-435.
A useful article for planning microform facilities. Discusses systems in four libraries, with photographs and floor plans.

Srygley, Sarah Krentzman. "Designing Facilities for School Library Materials Centers," *The School Library Materials Center: Its Resources and Their Utilization*, Alice Lohrer, ed. Champaign, IL: Illini Union Bookstore, 1964, 59-68. (Illinois University. Graduate School of Library Science, Allerton Park Institute, 10)

Problems of redesigning facilities during a period of rapid educational change. Discussion of the role of the librarian in the planning process. Papers presented at the Institute conducted by the University of Illinois Graduate School of Library Science, Nov. 3-6, 1963; remains timely.

Strassberg, Richard. *Conservation, Safety, Security, and Disaster Considerations in Designing New or Renovated Library Facilities at Cornell University Libraries*. Ithaca, NY: Cornell University Library, 1984. 10p.

An excellent paper, written for Cornell's needs, but of value to all institutions planning library or archive facilities.*

Thompson, Anthony. *Library Buildings of Britain and Europe; An Introductory Study*. London: Butterworths, 1963. 326p.

Written for the architect, with background material for the librarian, to provide basic information about the organization of libraries. Includes descriptions and illustrations.

Thompson, Anthony. "Library Planning: Principles and Plan Types," *Architects Journal*, 141:8 (Feb. 24, 1965), 493-500.

Outlines principles of library design, including ten based upon Soule. Includes a brief historical survey of library building types, explaining how each evolved.

Thompson, Godfrey. "Building for Libraries," *Manual of Library Economy: A Conspectus of Professional Librarianship for Students and Practitioners*, R. Northwood Lock, ed. London: Bingley; Hamden, CT: Linnet Books, 1977, 119-134.

A discussion of the elements in the planning process and working with the architect.

Thompson, Godfrey. *Planning and Design of Library Buildings*, 3rd ed. New York: Nichols, 1989. 232p.

A detailed discussion on planning and designing a library. Bibliography.

Toffler, Alvin. "Libraries," *Reader on the Library Building*, Hal
B. Schell, ed. Englewood, CO: Microcard Editions, 1975, 30-49.
  A futurist's look at the past and the future of libraries. Toffler
addresses the complexities of automation and offers a still-valid
reflection on the situation in libraries. Reprinted from *Bricks
and Mortarboards*. New York: Educational Facilities Laboratory, 1964.

Weber, David C, ed. "University Library Buildings," *Library
Trends*, 18:2 (Oct. 1969), 107-270.
  A collection of essays that deal with all aspects of library
planning.

Wilson, William K. "Standards and Specifications for Archival
Materials," *Restorator*, 3:4 (1979), 153-157.
  Describes the basic guidelines for a functioning archive. A
summary of the reports presented at the Preservation Methods
Committee, Society of American Archivists, Chicago, 1979.

The Library Consultant

(This list of readings specifically deals with the role of the
consultant in library planning.)

American Library Association. Library Administration and
Management Association. *Library Buildings Consultant List*.
Chicago: American Library Association. Updated frequently.
  A list of consultants prepared by the Library Administration
and Management Association.

Bierwirth, Ed. "When Retrofitting Build in the Degree of Fire
Protection Needed," *ASHRAE Journal*, 26:4 (April 1984), 48-49.
  Discusses how to analyze a building and work with a
consultant; especially useful for libraries adding more mechanical and technical facilities.

Corrigan, Dorothy D. and Hoyt R. Galvin. "Library Building
Consulting: Problems and Ethics," *ALA Bulletin*, 62:5 (May
1968), 505-510.
  The ethics of consulting; guidelines for the library board
and for consultants. Notes that a consultant "is usually a

librarian who has successful experience in library building planning."

DeProspo, Ernest R., Jr., ed. *The Library Building Consultant: Role and Responsibility; Report of a Seminar.* New Brunswick, NJ: Rutgers University Press, 1969. 110p.

The role of the consultant is discussed from sociological and practical aspects. Papers from a seminar for experienced building consultants held at Rutgers University in June 1968.

Ellsworth, Ralph E. "Consultants for College and University Library Building Planning," *College and Research Libraries*, 21:3 (July 1960), 263-268.

Brief historical sketch of the development of the library consultant as a member of the planning team. Describes the responsibilities of the consultant; details how to proceed with a program. Contains a model outline of a successful program written by Ellsworth Mason for the Colorado College Library.

Haas, Warren J. "The Role of the Building Consultant," *College and Research Libraries*, 40:3 (July 1969), 365-368.

Examines the role of the consultant from the development of the initial program through the production of the final design and the production of working drawings and specifications.

Mason, Ellsworth. "Consulting on Academic Library Buildings," *Library Trends*, 28:3 (Winter 1980), 363-380.

An excellent analysis of the consultant's role.

Metcalf, Keyes. "The Library Building Consultant," *Problems in Planning Library Facilities.* Chicago: American Library Association, 1964, 9-11; American Library Association *Bulletin*, 57:11 (Dec. 1963), 1043-1047.

Metcalf discusses the role of the consultant, selection and payment. A paper presented at the Library Buildings Institute, Chicago, 1963.

The Architect

(This selection of readings concentrates on the role of the architect in the planning process.)

Anderson, Harry F. "The Architect Views the Building and the Planning Process," *Junior College Libraries*, E.L. Moore, ed. Chicago: American Library Association, 1969, 95-99. (ACRL Monograph, 30)

Sound advice on preparing a program for an architect, with emphasis on designing the library for the user. Paper presented at a conference sponsored by the American Library Association, the American Association of Junior Colleges, and the University of California-Los Angeles.

Bailey, J. Russell. "Mr. Architect, Listen," *Library Journal*, 90:21 (Dec. 1, 1965), 5147-5151.

An article written by an architect for librarians on what patrons need; emphasizes that both architects and librarians have not been providing what the public wants.

Diamond, William E., II. "Business, Art, and Profession of Architecture," *Building Design and Construction Handbook*, 4th ed., Frederick S. Merritt, ed. New York: McGraw-Hill, 1982, 2/1-19.

Describes the role of the architect.

Feilden, Bernard M. *Conservation of Historic Buildings.* London: Butterworths, 1982. 448p.

Describes the role of the conservation architect, starting with the survey; includes the organization of work and the control of costs. A comprehensive survey of the fundamental principles of conservation and their application to historic buildings.

Gondos, Victor, Jr. "Collaboration Between Archivists and Architects in Planning Archives Buildings," *Bulletin of the National Archives*, 6 (June 1944), 157-169.

Practical information on the preservation of archival materials, which the author considers a fundamental of archives. Article appeared in a special issue, *Buildings and Equipment for Archives*.

Hilberry, John D., "What Architects Need to Know, and Don't Want to Hear," *Museum News*, 61:5 (June 1983), 55-61.

Describes, for the architect, a building program for a museum, with a reminder of the complexity of its design; libraries are comparable. Includes a "Checklist for Museum Building Programs," which covers all the services in a museum.

Hudnut, Joseph. "Architect and Librarian," *Library Quarterly,* 18:2 (April 1948), 93-99.

An architect's thoughts on the relationship between the architect and the librarian; reflects a reaction to the change in library style from the "monumental" to the "functional" which occurred at this time. Worth reading, as the "functionalist" approach to library planning is now being criticized.

McAdams, Nancy R. "Selecting an Architect for the Library," *Texas Library Journal,* 41:2 (Summer 1965), 38-43.

A clear statement of what an architect is and what he can do, written by an architect attending library school.

Schoenberner, Robert A. "What the Architect Needs to Know About the Archives," *American Archivist,* 27:4 (Oct. 1964), 491-493.

The architect's role in the planning and design of an archive repository.

Thompson, Carl. "The Architect and the Librarian," *UNESCO Bulletin for Libraries,* 16:3 (May-June 1962), 136-140.

The relationship between architect, librarian and builder.

The Contractor

(The articles listed below focus on the role of the contractor and the contracting engineer in the planning process.)

Fisher, Don. "The Changing Role of the Building Services Contractor," *Heating and Air Conditioning Journal,* 51:10 (Oct. 1975), 18-20.

Describes the traditional role of the contractor and discusses the need for him/her to become more actively involved with the architect and the client in the design and creation of a building.

Wright, N.O. "What the Construction Company Needs to Know About Archives," *American Archivist,* 27:4 (Oct. 1964), 495-497.

Stresses the need for the careful selection of all the people concerned with the construction of a building; the need for careful coordination between the architect and the sub-contracting forces, and the journeymen employed by the prime contractor; and the need to instill the importance of the building in the workers. This is one of the few articles on construction published in the professional literature.

CHAPTER 2. Design, Construction, and Renovation

INTRODUCTION

A S WE HAVE DISCUSSED EARLIER, the concepts of good library and archival planning and design have remained relatively constant over the centuries; their guiding principles are the collection, organization, preservation and dissemination of information. Only the style of the repository has changed to reflect the taste of the period in which it was designed. Each generation has criticized the buildings that have come before, but, in the main, most library buildings have worked reasonably well, both welcoming users and protecting their contents. Until this century, the care and preservation of collections were important factors in library and archive design because books, documents and other materials have not been as common as they are in today's world of mass publishing and reproduction. The records of society were highly valued.

One of the least satisfactory periods in library and archival design is a recent one, from the late 1940s until the 1970s and, to some extent, today, in an age of information and rapidly developing technologies. Although Angus Snead Macdonald and others had conceived of the modular, or "functional," library building before the war, it evolved in the 1940s; Macdonald unveiled his model at the Orange Conference in 1944. Most of these "functional" buildings have proven to be anything but functional, as librarians, archivists and architects, swept away in an enthusiasm for the new and awash with federal funds, did not bother, or did not know how, to consider how the user community functioned. But, like generations of critics before us, perhaps we are unduly harsh toward these postwar buildings, and another generation will find more of merit in their design. Many architectural critics have found the functionalism of the early postwar period beautiful in itself. Certainly these buildings stand as a reflection of the postwar enthusiasm and expansionism, when Americans felt that technology could solve everything. However, the fact is that for the first time the preservation of the collection, the very collection that the users came to consult, was paid scant attention. Library materials were considered expendable in a period of built-in obsolescence; if a book disintegrated, one could always purchase another, better book.

Ellsworth Mason has written:

> A building is a three-dimensional (not conceptual) solid masonry, and it will have a major visual impact on the community or campus for at least a hundred years. If it fails, we cannot return to what we were doing before, and can't call in a new consultant to rebuild it from scratch. It must be, in as many ways as possible, easily convertible to unforeseen uses to which it will be put over a century.[1]

Funds for libraries and archives are no longer as plentiful as they were from the postwar period to 1970. Proportionally fewer new facilities will be built in the years to come. Whether they were successful or not, the libraries and archive repositories that have been built in the past thirty or forty years must continue to suffice for the immediate future. Expansion and renovation, rather than the construction of new buildings, is common.

Library collections are no longer growing at the rapid rate they were in the postwar period. Although publishing continues to explode, librarians are realizing that bigger is not necessarily better and, further, that the replacement of basic materials is a very costly business. With the comparatively few dollars available to libraries and greater competition for those dollars, collection development is far more focused and selective. Collection management, a term that includes the care and preservation of library and archival materials, has become an important part of overall management strategy.

The readings selected for this section on library and archive buildings reflect the thoughts and experience of many people who have participated in the creation of library and archive buildings or who have had to live with the results of their creation. Many of these articles are illustrated. They do not represent the best advice, but they do reflect the body of information that has been given to librarians and archivists over the past half-century. For better or worse, this advice has had an influence on library planning and design. Modular structures have proven to be less flexible than anticipated; heating and ventilation systems are inadequate; curvilinear roofs, sunken gardens, skylights and picture windows have taken their toll on the materials as well as on the people who are obliged to work in such buildings. Studying the reasons for the design of an unfortunate building may not immediately present solutions to its problems. Some understanding of how such problems occurred, however, may help in the planning process for those who must live with such a building. For those fortunate enough to be able to plan new facilities, a review of the literature on library and archival building construction may help to clarify perspective prior to the commencement of the planning process. This section will cover building structure, renovation and the interior furnishings of the library or archives building.

STRUCTURE

Few, if any, librarians or archivists have had the technical training to enable them to work hand-in-hand with structural engineers and contractors during the planning and construction phases of a new or renovated building.

Yet, one of the principal causes of deterioration or structural failure is some relatively small carelessness or oversight in the details of design or in the construction of a building.[2] The library or archive administrator should know something about building structure, materials, construction and codes. Although it is unfortunate that courses on library planning, design and construction are not a mandatory part of the graduate library curriculum, there is no excuse for an administrator's neglect of these matters when planning for construction.

The very first consideration when planning a structure for a library or archive repository is the location and site of the building. These factors will dictate, to a significant degree, the design of the structure. The geographic location of the facility is an important factor. The architect and engineers who are designing the building must be aware of the codes that may minimize damage from natural disasters such as earthquakes, hurricanes and tornados that can occur in an area. However, the administrator should also be aware of these potential problems and should be able to discuss structural matters related to them with the architect and engineer.

The particular site of a building can offer further hazards. Is it to be near a river, such as the Johnstown (Pennsylvania) Public Library, or on the San Andreas fault, such as the Coalinga (California) Public Library? If the site itself presents problems, certain protective measures can be built into the structure, but this needs to be done as the building is being planned. Urban, suburban and rural sites each have their own particular set of problems that will affect the design of the structure.

Today most libraries and archives have flat roofs because they are cheaper to build. A flat roof will probably leak within a decade. It will need to be checked on a regular basis, and it will have to be replaced, like all roofs, within twenty years. Although it is possible to design buildings with slightly sloping roofs, it is usually more costly to do so. If it is decided that a flat roof will cover the building, rare, valuable and irreplaceable materials should not be placed below it. A good maintenance program will spot little problems before they become big ones; this should be planned for from the beginning.

Plumbing and heating pipes carry water, which is very harmful to all library and archival materials. The placement of plumbing and heating pipes must be carefully thought out in the planning and design phase of the building. If they are damaged, leaks can be devastating. It is the responsibility of the administrator to let the architect, engineer and construction people know how harmful water can be to the materials in the building. There are new materials for plumbing and heating continually coming on the market. Some are better, and cheaper; some are not. The administrator must discuss such problems and materials fully with the architect, engineer and contractors.

Traditional building materials have included stone, wood, brick, mortar and concrete. Today there is a broad spectrum of materials that can be used. Each has its strengths and weaknesses. Each will respond to its environment by expanding and contracting, emitting moisture and pollutants. There is no ideal material for the construction of a library or archive, nor is there a material that is especially harmful. Location, site, needs and the design will help dictate the materials to be used in construction. The administrator should find out about the nature of these materials, which can be done through reading and through continued questioning and discussion with the architect, engineers, contractors and the community's planning office.

The administrator should be aware of the rapidly changing nature of the heating, ventilating and air conditioning (HVAC) industry. The technology is moving rapidly, and not all new developments are proving to be better, or even good. Computerized systems are subject to breakdowns. Air filtration systems are tricky, and discussion of many inherent problems are emerging in the HVAC literature. (This topic will be addressed more fully in Chapter 4.) Once again, if the architect, engineer, and contractors are made aware of the special needs of libraries and archives and the requirements that are necessary for the care of the collections, pitfalls that can prove very costly may be avoided.

A sound rule when building or renovating a facility is for the client to be there and to ask questions. Master the vocabulary of the architect, the engineer and the construction crews and hope that they will master some of our special vocabulary. The bibliography on structure will supply basic information about the building and construction industry, problems in construction and materials, and some general information. Because the technology in the building industry is changing so rapidly, making an effort to keep up with some of the trade journals is important. These provide specific technical information about new products and materials in a timely manner. Spending a brief period of time to glance through them can prove very helpful.

Every change that is made during construction will cost money. It is best, of course, to make changes in the design before construction begins. These are the least expensive. Attention to detail will lead to a successful building—one that is attractive, that suitably houses the materials in it and is truly functional for its users.

RENOVATION

If the library or archive is to be renovated or if an addition is to be built, a survey of the building beforehand is of critical importance. The structure must be studied to determine the most appropriate and cost-effective construction. This is the time to take measures to protect against future problems and also to protect against hazards that can occur during construction. Library and archival literature is filled with case studies of disasters that occurred in operating repositories during construction.

There are a number of elements in the building survey that need to be studied. To begin, it is necessary to have a complete set of plans for the building. These should have been made available to the institution at the time the original building was completed. They should show the nature of the structure and the placement of plumbing, heating, air conditioning and electrical systems. It is also necessary to consider the history of the structure. How old is the building? Has it ever had fire or water damage? If so, were the causes eliminated or only patched up?

The placement of the heating plant, electrical system and plumbing should be reviewed. The heating plant should be adequately cut off from the rest of the building by walls, floor, and ceiling, each with the appropriate fire-resistance rating. Openings that connect the building with the heating plant should be properly protected with fire doors. Openings for pipes and ducts must be sealed appropriately. The heating plant should have the capacity to heat the original building and newly constructed areas without taxing the system. A new or augmented heating plant may be necessary. Fuel should not be stored in the building; it should be piped in. Fuses and circuit breakers should provide protection. The circuitry for electrical systems should be planned so that it does not become overloaded as a result of the addition of new technical equipment, such as computer terminals. Although computer terminals are low amperage items, there are often many of them in an area for a high cumulative load. There should never be any temporary wiring. Plumbing should never pass above or near areas where library and archival materials are stored.

The roof should be carefully examined, and there should be adequate drainage. Skylights are inappropriate for library and archive buildings (see Chapter 4). They should not be a part of a renovation. If they exist in the older structure, it is a good time to eliminate them. Although many library and archive buildings have sealed windows, they should be checked to see that they are tight. Collections of library and archival materials should not be placed near windows where they can be exposed to the hazard of ultra-violet light.

Concealed spaces, areas between floors and pipe chases, are especially hazardous because fire can travel through them, spreading throughout a structure until the flames burst out. They should be eliminated, whenever possible, or made safe at the time of renovation. Walls between floors and pipe chases should be fire-stopped; fire walls and fire partitions should extend through the roof. This will usually be covered by the building code. Library and archive repositories should have only as many exits as are necessary for safety and security. These are required by the building code and, in many states, a fire protection code. Exits should be clearly marked and unimpeded by electronic security systems. Emergency lighting must be on separate circuits or battery powered. General storage areas should be adequately lit.

Fire protection systems should be installed, then properly maintained. Automatic sprinkler systems are required by law in some institutions and their design has improved considerably over the past decade. However, they cannot be recommended unequivocally. Their installation requires careful consideration, and their presence in a repository requires special emergency planning. Although fire extinguishers, placed in convenient places, are sometimes required, some fire experts recommend against them because, when improperly operated, they can cause more harm than good. Working with the local fire department during the planning stage of an addition or renovation is important and will establish relationships that can prove critical should an emergency occur.

The extensive use of asbestos in postwar buildings has created serious problems that must be considered when the renovation of such a building is planned. Asbestos can be found nearly everywhere—on piping and ducts, in ceilings, in floors. As we are learning, asbestos is a substance that can be extremely hazardous to health. It is known as a "ticking time bomb" because in time it will break down, and it is the asbestos particles in the air that cause harm to people. Buildings with loose asbestos will need to be cleaned for renovation. It is a costly business, as the workers who remove asbestos must be protected from contamination by the fibers and the asbestos must be disposed of following the strict guidelines of the Occupational Safety and Health Administration (OSHA), the

Environmental Protection Agency (EPA) and state regulations. The need for asbestos removal may trigger a more
thorough renovation of building space. There is no
question that renovation forced by an asbestos problem
will be of considerable cost and that service will be
disrupted during its removal. Administrators are urged to
learn about asbestos and to become familiar with the
legislation concerning its elimination. The presence of
asbestos in libraries and in archive repositories may prove
to be one of the administrator's most difficult problems in
the next decade.

NOTES

1. "Consulting on Academic Library Buildings," *Library
   Trends,* 28:3 (Winter 1980), 363.
2. Sidney M. Johnson. *Deterioration, Maintenance, and Repair
   of Structures.* NY: McGraw-Hill, 1965, 11.

BIBLIOGRAPHY

General References

Allen, Walter C. "Library Buildings," *Library Trends,* 25:1 (July
1976), 89-112.
   This article examines "a century of library architecture in
relation to changing perceptions of library functions, the
development of building techniques and materials, fluctuating
aesthetic fashions, and sometimes wildly erratic economic
climates."

Burchard, John E., Charles W. David and Julian P. Boyd.
*Planning the University Library Building: a Summary of
Discussions by Librarians, Architects and Engineers.* Princeton,
NJ: Princeton University Press, 1949. 145p.
   The report of the Cooperative Committee on Library Building
Plans, prepared at the beginning of the postwar period when
institutions of higher education were rapidly expanding. Dis-
cussion focuses on flexibility, adaptability, expansion and

growth in libraries. This report provided a framework for library planning and design for the next quarter of a century.

Crosbie, Michael J. "Library Science: Planning for Book Conservation, Storage, and Information Retrieval," *Architecture (AIA)*, 79:7 (July 1990), 103-105.
Discusses environmental control and storage for libraries containing printed and electronic information media.

Duchein, Michel. *Archives Buildings and Equipment*. Munich: Verlag Dokumentation, 1977. 201p. (ICA Handbook Series, 1)
Covers all aspects of construction and renovation of archives and a concern for the preservation of the material is reflected throughout. A supplemented translation of *Les Batiments et Equipements d'Archives* (Paris 1966), sponsored by the International Council on Archives.*

Ernestus, Horst and Engelbert Plassmann. *Libraries in the Federal Republic of Germany*, 2nd ed., rev. and enl. Wiesbaden: Harrasowitz, 1983. 288p.
Provides information on a variety of library types. Updated, with sections rewritten of the 1968 edition, edited by Gisela Von Busse and Ernestus. (English edition, 1972)

Freeman, Michael S. "College Library Buildings in Transition: A Study of 36 Libraries Built in 1967-68," *College and Research Libraries*, 43:6 (Nov. 1982), 478-480.
The author examined institutions with enrollment under 3,000 to see how well they have adapted and serve their constituents; observes that space is the most critical problem these libraries face in the 1980s.

Institute on Public Library Architecture, Los Angeles, 1957. *A Living Library; Planning Public Library Buildings for Cities of 100,000 or Less*, Martha Boaz, ed. Los Angeles: University of Southern California Press, 1957. 84p.
Papers cover planning, site selection, building services offered, engineering and structural details, with information on blueprint reading and cost analyses.

Jones, Harold D. "Recent Trends in West German University Library Planning," *College and Research Libraries*, 42:5 (Sept. 1981), 461-469.

A capsule survey of several libraries constructed in the past decade.

Kaser, David. "Twenty-five Years of Academic Building Planning," *College and Research Libraries*, 45:4 (July 1984), 268-281.
A distinguished library consultant discusses the evolution of the modular design concept over the past 25 years, observing that it originally lent itself well to efficient library operations. However, modifications in the design work to the detriment of libraries, hindering workflow and causing problems with heating, ventilation and lighting. Kaser observes that underground libraries have had no more problems with water leakage than traditional buildings; they may be sounder than the flat-roof building.

Library Association. *New Library Buildings*. London: 1973 to date.
From 1973 the Library Association (United Kingdom) has published a series of annual volumes surveying new libraries designed and constructed during the preceding year.

Macdonald, Angus Snead. "Some Comments on Modular Buildings," *Proceedings of the Fifth and Sixth Library Building Plans Institutes*. Chicago: Association of College and Research Libraries, 1955, 155-157.
The inventor of modular construction for library buildings explains how to apply it successfully. "Modular construction is not purely physical; it should be directed by a philosophy which aims towards the removal of constriction on library functions and provides for future expansion."

Mason, Ellsworth. "Back to the Cave; or Some Buildings I Have Known," *Library Journal*, 94:21 (Dec. 1969), 4353-4357.
Cites examples of mistakes that were made in specific libraries and offers suggestions on how to avoid them in the future.

Mason, Ellsworth. "Balbus; or the Future of Library Buildings," *Farewell to Alexandria*, Daniel Gore, ed. Westport, CT: Greenwood Press, 1975, 22-33.
A criticism of buildings constructed in the recent past and a discussion of the impact of the energy shortage on libraries and

new technology. Mason predicts that library buildings will be constricted in the future.

Mason, Ellsworth. *Mason on Library Buildings*. Metuchen, NJ: Scarecrow Press, 1980. 333p.
A collection of the distinguished library consultant and critic's papers. The volume provides an excellent foundation for the understanding of library buildings.*

Merritt, Frederick S., ed. *Building Design and Construction Handbook*, 4th ed. New York: McGraw-Hill, 1982. 1479p.
A compendium of the best of current building design and construction practices; information to assist on the selection of building materials and construction methods. Originally published as the *Building Construction Handbook*.

Metcalf, Keyes DeWitt. *Planning Academic and Research Library Buildings*. New York: McGraw-Hill, 1965. 431p.
Metcalf's classic study on library buildings. It still contains much practical information on the planning and construction of all types of library buildings.*

Metcalf, Keyes DeWitt. *Planning Academic and Research Library Buildings*, 2nd ed. by Philip D. Leighton and David C. Weber. Chicago: American Library Association, 1986. 630p.
This edition has been rewritten to deal with the problems that new materials and technologies have created for library planners since Metcalf published the first edition. While Metcalf could only recognize their coming in 1966, Leighton and Weber have had to deal with them. There are no longer as many absolutes in planning libraries, and this excellent text discusses the many issues that need to be faced clearly and lucidly.*

Metcalf, Keyes DeWitt. "Selection of Library Sites," *College and Research Libraries*, 23:3 (May 1961), 183-192.
Selecting a site, with attention paid to environmental considerations.

Orr, J.M. *Designing Library Buildings for Activity*. London: Deutsch, 1972. 152p.
A basic textbook on library design with the preservation of the collections stressed throughout.

Sanchez Belda, Luis. "Construction of Archives Buildings in the Last Ten Years," *UNESCO Bulletin for Libraries,* 18:1 (Jan.-Feb. 1964), 20-26. Illus.

A general account of European archives buildings, focusing on structures that offer protection for collections.

Srygley, Sara Krentzman. "Designing Facilities for School Library Materials Centers," *The School Library Materials Center: Its Resources and Their Utilization,* Alice Lohrer, ed. Champaign, IL: Illini Union Bookstore, 1964, 59-68.

Discusses the problems of redesigning facilities at a period of rapid change in education. Paper presented at an Institute conducted by the University of Illinois Graduate School of Library Science, November 1963.

Thompson, Anthony. *Library Buildings of Britain and Europe; An Introductory Study.* London: Butterworths, 1963. 326p.

Written for the architect to provide basic information about the organization of libraries, with background material for librarians. Included are descriptions of what the author considers to be good library design.

Thompson, Donald E. "Education for Building," *Library Journal,* 90:21 (Dec. 1, 1965), 5157-5160.

Offers the suggestion that courses on library building, equipment and purchasing should be included in graduate programs.

Thompson, Godfrey. *Planning and Design of Library Buildings,* 3rd ed. New York: Nichols, 1989. 232p.

A thorough discussion on planning and designing a library. Bibliography.

Weber, David C., ed. "University Library Buildings," *Library Trends,* 18:2 (Oct. 1969), 107-270.

A collection of essays on library planning.

Wise, Douglass. "Specification for Minimal Maintenance," *International Journal of Museum Management and Curatorship,* 3:4 (Dec. 1984), 357-362.

An excellent article on the planning of buildings to curtail maintenance costs. Practical advice on the planning process as well as on roofing, the shell, the interior and the mechanical systems.*

Wynne, G.B. *Building Estimating*. Columbus, OH: Merrill, 1973. 320p.

The author introduces principles, theories and procedures involved in building and construction cost estimating, and discusses the factors governing the cost of construction materials. Covers excavation, concrete, structural steel, masonry, wood and laminated construction, moisture protection, glazing, finished pre-fabricated materials and mechanical equipment.

Structure

AI Handbook of Building Structure 2/e, ed. Allan Hodgkinson. New York: Nichols, 1980. 400p.

Reviews the structural field, with sections on movement in buildings, fire protection, structural legislation, foundations and specific structural materials.

Addleston, Lyall. *Building Failures: A Guide to Diagnosis, Remedy and Prevention*. 2nd ed., rev. London: Butterworths, 1990. 176p. Illus.

A guide to diagnosis, remedy and prevention of non-structural failures due to damp, movement and chemical/biological changes that may lead to structural and envelope deterioration. Discusses how they may be overcome at the design stage and when they occur afterward. Clearly written; bibliography.*

Allen, Bill. "Building Defects—What Went Wrong," *Architects Journal*, 179:50 (Dec. 14, 1983), 63-66.

A discussion of the defects discovered in post-World War II buildings. The author explains how situations occurred and identifies fundamental issues that should be resolved.

American Institute of Architects. *The Building Systems Integration Handbook*, Richard Rush, ed. New York: Wiley, 1986. 445p. Illus.

Examines the integration of systems within buildings from a variety of perspectives, theoretical and practical.

Arnold, Christopher. "In Earthquakes, Failure Can Follow Form," *AIA Journal* (American Institute of Architects), 69:6 (June 1980), 33-41.

A clear discussion of the need to assess the seismatic influence when planning the configuration of a building in an unstable area. Explains why some buildings have failed.

Ashley, R. *Electrical Estimating*. New York: McGraw-Hill, 1961. 437p.
A manual containing information required to estimate the cost of any electrical contracting job from beginning to conclusion.

Brookes, Alan and Chris Grech. *The Building Envelope: Applications of New Technology Cladding*. New York: Nichols, 1990. 192p.
Describes advanced construction and new materials. Case studies.

Building Practices for Disaster Mitigation, ed. Richard Wright, Samuel Kramer and Charles Culver. Washington, DC: National Bureau of Standards, 1973. 474p.
Presents recommendations for planning and construction to curtail the consequences of natural disasters. Technical papers with bibliographies. Proceedings of a workshop sponsored by the National Science Foundation Research Applied to National Needs Program and the National Bureau of Science.*

"Durability of Concrete," *The Consulting Engineer*, Supplement. 5:4 (April-May 1971), 32p.
Contains 8 articles on the causes of decay, durability, design and workmanship.

Eagleman, J. R. (et al.) *Thunderstorms, Tornados, and Building Damage*. Lexington, MA: Lexington, 1975. 317p.
Discussion of design and construction practices that minimize storm damage.

Fischer, Robert E. and James B. Gardner. "Modern Wiring Systems: An Innovative and Maturing Technology," *Architectural Record*, 170:10 (Oct. 1982), 134-141. Illus.
A brief introduction to new technological developments to deal with electronic innovations in the workplace.*

Fischer, Robert E. "Round Table: Concrete in Architecture, A Current Assessment," *Architectural Record*, 170:11 (Nov. 1982), 122-129.

A discussion of the merits and problems of concrete as a building material.

Fisher, Thomas. "Designer Roofs," *Progressive Architecture,* 67:7 (July 1986), 120-125.
Discusses recent changes in roofing technology and products.

Fisher, Thomas. "Making Ends Meet," *Progressive Architecture,* 66:2 (Feb. 1985), 105-110.
Describes the variety of materials that can be used in the joints of buildings. The need to have the joints carefully designed is emphasized.

Fisher, Thomas. "The Watery Underworld," *Progressive Architecture,* 66:10 (Oct. 1985), 105-109.
Describes a variety of methods for the waterproofing of underground areas.

Garvin, John D. "Windows: Factors to Consider Before Buying," *American School and University,* 47:7 (March 1975), 18-20.
Surveys different kinds of windows used in college buildings, and the pros and cons of each.

Genge, G.R. "Roofing and Waterproofing Update," *Canadian Architect,* 32:7 (July 1987), 47-49.
Brief discussion of good design practice for flat commercial roofs. The need for a careful consideration of the variety of materials available is emphasized.

Godel, Jules B. *Sources of Construction Information,* vol. 1: *Books.* Metuchen, NJ: Scarecrow Press, 1977. 661p.
An annotated guide to reports, books, periodicals, standards and codes; covers major sources of information, including planning, management, design, materials, construction, the industry, and selected topics, including fire safety and general safety and security.*

Griffin, Charles Williams. *Manual of Built-up Roof Systems,* 2nd ed. New York: McGraw-Hill, 1982. 484p. Illus.
Provides comprehensive data on every component of the roof system: deck, vapor retarder, insulation, membrane, and flashing, as well as essential information on roof drainage, wind uplift, fire resistance, specifications, bonds and guarantees, and field inspection.*

Hallanger, Erling. "Pressure and Flow Control in Hot and Chilled Water Piping," *Heating/Piping/Air Conditioning*, 54:10 (Oct. 1982), 55-59.
Basic information about hydraulic plumbing systems and their problems.

Institute on Public Library Architecture, Los Angeles, 1957. *A Living Library: Planning Public Library Buildings for Cities of 100,000 or Less*, Martha Boaz, ed. Los Angeles: University of Southern California Press, 1957. 84p.
Topics include the structural details of buildings, cost analysis and blueprint reading.

Janney, Jack R. *Guide to Investigation of Structural Failures.* New York: American Society of Civil Engineers, 1979. 76p.
A guide "to aid the investigating engineer in determining the cause of structural failure," and a suggested format for documentation in the investigation. The volume was written for professional civil engineers, sponsored by the American Society of Chemical Engineers (ASCE) Research Council on Performance of Standards.

Kurtz, Norman D. "Engineering in the Information Age," *Progressive Architecture*, (67:4), 124-126.
A capsule review of the changes in technology that will affect the form and performance of buildings.*

Lieff, M. and H.R. Trechsel, eds. *Moisture Migration in Buildings.* Philadelphia: American Society for Testing and Materials, 1982. 293p. (ASTM Special Technical Publication, 779)
Technical papers dealing with roofing, walls, standards and tests, etc., with explanations for moisture problems.

Macmillan, Marc. *Pathology of Building Materials, Part 1: Stone; Part 2: Terracotta Materials, Coatings, Mortars.* Rome: International Centre for the Study of Preservation and the Restoration of Cultural Property, 1970. 53p.
Brief, clear information on the nature of these materials and how to care for them.

Marsh, Paul. *Thermal Insulation and Condensation.* London: Construction Press, 1979. 143p.

Discusses the problems caused by the energy crisis and the increasing interest in insulation. Excellent discussion of condensation in buildings.*

Merritt, Frederick S., ed. *Building Design and Construction Handbook*, 4th ed. New York: McGraw-Hill, 1982. 1479p.
A compendium of the best of current building design and construction practices, information useful for those making decisions affecting the selection of building materials and construction methods. The emphasis is on fundamental principles and their potential application.*

Messman, Howard A. *Building Materials in Library Construction*. Urbana: University of Illinois Graduate School of Library Science, 1963. 23p. (Occasional Papers, 67)
Covers foundations and footings, framework, roofing, subfloors, window frames, sheet work metal, glass and glazing, painting, woodwork, finishing hardware, exterior walls, interior walls. Bibliography.*

Mills, Edward D., ed. *Building Maintenance and Preservation: A Guide for Design and Management*. London: Butterworths/ The Building Centre Trust, 1980. 203p.
A concise but comprehensive volume covering all aspects of building maintenance as an extension of the life of a building. Although prepared to meet problems in Great Britain, there is much of relevance for American readers. Emphasis on awareness of maintenance issues at the design phase.

National Materials Advisory Board. Committee on Conservation of Historic Buildings and Monuments. *Conservation of Historic Stone Buildings and Monuments*. Washington, DC: National Academy Press, 1982. 365p.
Provides clearly written information on structural decay. Proceedings of a conference to summarize the state of research on stone conservation, to define research needs and priorities, and to interest scientists in studying the problems at hand.

Oliver, Alan C. *Dampness in Buildings*. New York: Nichols, 1988. 232p. Illus.
Covers materials, design and construction in relation to moisture exclusion and techniques of diagnosis.

Oxley, T.A. and E.G. Gobert. *Dampness in Buildings: Diagnosis, Treatment, Instruments.* London: Butterworths, 1983. 132p.
   A guide to the nature of dampness, how to diagnose it before it gets out of hand, and how to deal with it. The author writes, "By the time you can see and feel a dampness problem in a building, you are usually in the presence of a major failure of the building. . . . Wood becomes visibly damp at between 30-40% moisture content. Yet serious decay will occur at 20 or 22%."

Paul Tente Associates. *Roofing: Concepts/Principles, A Practical Approach to Roofing,* 2nd ed. Colorado Springs, CO: Paul Tente Associates, 1980. 39p. Illus.
   Written for those who write roofing specifications or are involved in the selection of materials or systems. Brief, clearly written and filled with practical advice.

Ransom, W.H. *Building Failures: Diagnosis and Avoidance.* London: Spon, 1981. 174p.
   Identifies the nature and cause of important defects occurring in buildings, with emphasis on those affecting the fabric of a building. Covers causes of deterioration, durability of materials, moisture, foundations, flooring, walls, cladding, doors and windows, roofs, heating and plumbing, and causes and control of failures. Written for the builder or architect, but provides clearly written information for the layperson.

Robertson, Larry. "Roof Drainage Systems," *Heating/Piping/Air Conditioning,* 60:4 (May 1988), 81-84,89-91.
   A discussion of considerations and design that should assure proper roof drainage.

Roofing Materials Reference Guide. Rosemont, IL: Roofing Contractors Association, published 3 times a year.
   Covers all built-up and sheet-applied roofing products, giving general information on manufacturers and technical data on test results.

Rosen, Harold J. *Construction Materials for Architecture.* New York: Wiley, 1985. 233 p. Illus. (Wiley Series of Practical Construction Guides)
   Covers sitework, concrete, masonry, metals, woodwork, thermal and moisture protection, glass and curtain walls, and finishes. Chapter 1, "Performance Considerations," outlines a

rational method of evaluating and selecting materials. Clearly written and illustrated; bibliography.*

Ross, Steven S. *Construction Disasters: Design Failures, Causes and Prevention.* New York: McGraw-Hill, 1984. 417p.
   A history of major structural failures of the 20th century. Explores what went wrong and how much progress has been made; why some lessons have not yet been learned; what steps must be taken to prevent future disasters.

Rush, Richard. "Building in the Path of Nature's Wrath," *Progressive Architecture,* 61:2 (Feb. 1980), 106-114.
   Reviews developments in construction that have evolved from structural failures caused by natural disasters in the hope that the knowledge gained will be integrated into design, planning and building codes.

Stavely, H.S. and P.V. Glover. *Surveying Buildings.* London: Butterworths, 1983. 240p.
   Guide to the principles and practice of building inspection. Covers structural and non-structural building elements.

Stone Decay and Conservation; Atmospheric Pollution, Cleaning, Consolidation and Protection. New York: Elsevier, 1983. 453p. (Materials Science Monograph, 1)
   A detailed study on the conservation and restoration of stone in historical, archaeological, and artistic buildings and monuments. Conservation techniques, scientific investigations and environmental problems are discussed as are the chemical and physical properties of polymeric substances available for treatment. Bibliographies and case histories.

Symposium on Roofing Technology, Proceedings. Gaithersburg, MD, Sept. 1977. Washington, DC: National Bureau of Standards/National Roofing Contractors Association, 1977. 282p.
   An exchange of information concerning new technologies in roofing and a discussion of the problems associated with roofing.

Thomas, Rose. "Major Changes Hit Both Camps of the Roofing Industry," *Building and Design Construction,* 24:5 (Aug. 1983), 104-107.

Discussion of trends in the use of new materials and techniques in the roofing industry.

Torraca, Giorgio. *Porous Building Materials: Materials Science for Architectural Conservation.* 3rd ed. Rome: International Centre for the Conservation and Restoration of Cultural Materials, 1988. 160p.

Chapters 1-5 present a general model of deterioration processes, including mechanical, physical, chemical and biological factors. Chapters 6-9 are devoted to masonry technology, including mortars, and general principles of conservation technology. Chapters 10-11 discuss modern materials used in conservation. A list of selected technical literature is given in each chapter.

Ulrey, Harry F. *Building Construction and Design.* Indianapolis, IN: Audel, 1970. 390p.

Written for the builder and the building designer to supply the information needed to avoid or correct common building faults directly affected by natural phenomena. It is geared toward home construction, but contains excellent discussion on heating, temperature, humidity, air pollution, and methods of controlling them. There is also excellent discussion on solar heating, light, acoustics, air and wind pressure, fire and water. The book provides a clear discussion of the factors that make good building construction for the preservation of people, buildings and materials.*

U.S. General Services Administration. Public Buildings Service. *Earthquake Resistance of Buildings.* Vol. 1: *Design Guidelines;* vol. 2: *Evaluation of Existing Structures.* Washington, DC: Govt. Print. Off., 1978. 56p; 51p. Illus.

Vol. 1 lists the guidelines that can be used in the structural design or evaluation of buildings. Vol. 2 presents a method for determining how well existing buildings can resist different degrees of seismatic activity.

U.S. National Bureau of Standards. Building Research Division. *Building Science Series.* Washington, DC: 1960 to present.

Disseminates technical information developed at the National Bureau of Standards on building materials, components, systems, and structures. Supercedes the National Bureau of Standards *Building Materials and Structures Reports,* 1938-1959.

Wagner, Walter F. and Robert E. Fischer, eds. "Round Table: Steel Structures in Architecture: Trends and New Developments," *Architectural Record,* 169:6 (June 1983), 104-111.

The discussion, co-sponsored with members from the American Iron and Steel Institute, focuses on fire, wind and earthquake safety.

Watson, John A. *Commercial Roofing Systems.* Reston, VA: Reston, 1984. 233p.

A discussion of commercial roofing systems and the problems that they can present, especially when roofing is not done properly. Clearly written, with glossary and sources of further information.

Williams, G.P. *Drainage around Buildings.* Ottawa: National Research Council of Canada, Division of Building Research, 1973. 4p. (Canadian Building Digest, 156)

A short general outline which describes the principles of good drainage practice.

Wilson, Forest. "Doctors for Sick Buildings," *Technology Review,* 89 (May-June 1986), 48-58.

Describes the new science of building diagnostics to improve the health of structures and the people within. Analyzes why buildings fail, citing the problem of complex mechanical systems and materials used in cleaning.*

Restoration and Renovation

Association of Research Libraries. Office of Management Studies. *Building Renovation in ARL Libraries.* Washington, DC: 1983. 99p. (SPEC Kit, 97)

Contains examples of a variety of planning and final report documents and a list of libraries contacted for this information.

Beckerman, Edwin P. "Planning and Construction of Buildings," *Local Public Library Administration,* 2nd rev. ed., Ellen Altman, ed. Chicago: American Library Association, 1980, 213-224.

Discussion of the problems that arise when renovating library buildings; a sound, common-sense approach.

GUIDE TO THE LITERATURE

Bullock, Orin M., Jr. *The Restoration Manual, An Illustrated Guide to the Preservation and Restoration of Old Buildings.* Norwalk, CT: Silvermine, 1966. 188p.
A basic guide that covers problems that are encountered in the renovation and rehabilitation of older buildings.

Cantacuzino, Sherban. *New Uses for Old Buildings.* New York: Whitney Library of Design, 1975. 264p.
Examples of adaptive re-use of buildings, including two libraries and an archive repository.

Dewe, Michael, ed. *Adaptation of Buildings to Library Use.* New York, Munich: Saur, 1988. 254p. (IFLA Publications, 39)
Papers on conversion, with case studies. Proceedings of a seminar held in Budapest, Hungary, June 1985.

Ellsworth, Ralph E. "The ABCs of Remodeling/Enlarging an Academic Library Building: A Personal Statement," *Journal of Academic Librarianship,* 7:6 (Jan. 1982), 334-343.
Discusses when a renovation of a building is possible and how to work with the architect and consultant. Case studies with plans.

Feilden, Bernard M. *Conservation of Historic Buildings.* London: Butterworths, 1982. 488 p. (Technical Studies in the Arts, Archaeology and Architecture)
A comprehensive survey of the fundamental principles of conservation in their application to historic buildings. Covers the structural aspects of historic buildings, causes of decay in materials and structure, the work of the conservation architect, building repairs, and special techniques.**

Hammond, Jay. "Adaptive Reuse of Old Buildings for Archives," *American Archivist,* 45:1 (Winter, 1982), 11-18.
A discussion of the benefits and challenges of moving collections into renovated space, with focus on environmental problems and solutions.

Holt, Raymond M., ed. *An Architectural Strategy for Change: Remodeling and Expanding for Contemporary Public Library Needs.* Chicago: American Library Association, 1976. 149p.
Discussion on specific library remodelling projects and how library development and renovation can interact.*

Markus, Thomas A. ed. *Building Conversion and Rehabilitation: Designing for Change in Building Use.* London: Newnes-Butterworths, 1979. 178p.

The volume is concerned with the problems associated with the continuous reuse of older buildings. Chapter 8: "Conservation or Renewal; A Study of the Library at Blackburn," by Keith Scott, pp. 120-131, deals with the conversion of an older structure into a public library.

Massey, James C. *The Architectural Survey.* Washington, DC: National Trust for Historic Preservation, c1969. 19p.

Explains how to undertake a survey of an historic property. Bibliography.

Metcalf, Keyes. "Problems of Renovating an Existing Library Building," *Running Out of Space—What Are the Alternatives?* Chicago: American Library Association, 1978, 97-101.

Eleven suggestions for planning for renovation, with some emphasis on the preservation of library materials. The mechanical system and lighting are discussed.

Nardini, Robert F. "The Asbestos Hazard in Libraries," *Library Journal,* 109:18 (Nov. 1, 1984), 2001-04.

An overview of the problem, with sources of information and assistance. The removal process from the physical and psychological perspective is discussed.

Streit, Samuel A. and Roberta G. Sautter. "Brown Renovation for Preservation," *Conservation Administration News,* no. 10 (July 1982), 1-4.

An analysis of the renovation of a Carnegie library building, with a concern for library materials as well as security.

Codes and Standards

American Society for Testing Materials. *Standards in Building Codes.* Philadelphia: ASTM, latest edition.

Includes all ASTM standards adopted in building codes throughout the United States and Canada; authentic sources of test procedures that serve as a basis for acceptable quality for materials and construction.

Building Officials and Code Administrators International Inc.
BOCA National Building Code. Country Club Hills, IL: BOCA;
updated every three years.

   Includes sample and model building codes for every state
which are nationally recognized standards for performance-
based construction methods and building components.

CHAPTER 3. The Interior: Shelving, Storage, Interior Design, and Exhibition Space

INTRODUCTION

THIS CHAPTER WILL DEAL WITH the topic of equipping and furnishing the interior of the library or archive, from shelving to sofas. It will also provide sources of information on storage facilities, a topic becoming ever more timely as space runs out in the library or archive building before funds for new facilities become available. Finally, it will provide information on exhibition space, as that is another increasingly popular feature in libraries and archives and an important part of an institution's outreach program.

The bibliography contains readings on interior design of the library which should be supplemented by the books and articles cited in Chapter 4, which deals with the technical aspects of providing a comfortable environment for both people and materials. An attractive, workable environment can be provided that is not harmful for library and archival materials.

SHELVING AND STORAGE

Inadequate shelving has been a continuing problem for librarians. It became acute in the nineteenth century with the rapid growth of the publishing industry and the expansion of the reading public. Cast-iron book stacks superceded the traditional cabinets of wood, only to be replaced by those made of steel. Prior to World War II, library book collections doubled every 25 years.[1] Until quite recently academic library collections doubled every seven years. The demand for information is greater than ever before in libraries and archives. Today's librarians and archivists are responsible not only for the housing of books, newspapers, maps and documents; they must also house a wide variety of materials in formats such as computer disk, magnetic tape, video and audio cassette, and film.

The information explosion has forced librarians and archivists to take a closer look at the storing of these resources. In the past two decades there has been a dramatic rise in the cost of buildings that house these massive collections. Shelving is one of the largest expenses of a library or archive. It deserves very careful consideration in the planning of a new facility or in the renovation of space. Yet, the body of useful literature on the subject is limited; the profession is still depending for information upon articles published well over a decade ago. The literature has not dealt adequately with possibilities offered by newer construction technologies. Although many shelving structures are experimental, as was Labrouste's structure for the Bibliothèque Sainte-Geneviève a century ago, adaptation for library and archival facilities usually can be done successfully.

The library or archive administrator need not be an expert in the details of shelving. What is important is that he or she knows what questions to ask of the vendor and the architect. A number of the articles in the bibliography deal with this aspect of interior planning. Leighton and Weber's revision of Keyes Metcalf's classic, *Planning the Academic Library Building* (1986), offers a considered discussion on shelving that is relevant for planners of all library buildings. Key elements of shelving schemes are costs (present and future), flexibility of space, control and access. The importance of these elements must be emphasized to the architect.

Collections are changing more rapidly than design and opinions; computers are playing an increasingly important role in library and archival operations. As space becomes more precious, microforms become more important, and administrators are inquiring about the potential of optical disc technology for storing and retrieving information. Libraries and archives that house non-traditional media are faced with new storage challenges. These media take up additional space and require specially designed equipment for storage and access.

Compact storage is an increasingly popular option for the housing of burgeoning collections. By the end of the last century, librarians were experimenting with movable shelves. "Sliding press" movable bookshelves were in operation in the British Museum by 1891.[2] These shelves remained in operation for many years with little problem, as long as they were properly maintained and books were carefully removed and replaced.

Fremont Rider, in his book, *Compact Book Storage*, published in 1949, recommended the arrangement of books by size. He also suggested that the width of the aisles in the stack area be narrowed to gain shelving space in little-used areas, and provided calculations for doing so. By the early 1950s, compact storage systems became relatively common. A number of manufacturers, including Snead and Company, supplied it. Today a variety of compact shelving systems that can be designed to suit an institution's needs are available.

Not only does compact shelving save valuable space, it can also save lighting, heating and air conditioning costs, as well as provide an excellent environment for the storage of infrequently used collections. However, it is not as successfully used in areas open to the public. The merits of compact shelving are discussed in a number of articles in the bibliography. The decision to install it and the way in which it is installed will depend upon the nature of the institution, its collection and its use, and the relative need for space.

A topic related to the compact storage of library and archival materials is the recent trend toward the construction of off-site storage facilities with a form of compact shelving. As the cost of building new facilities or renovating older ones escalates, the construction of an inexpensive warehouse facility is indeed appealing to institutions where land is more available than money. These facilities usually promise delivery of needed materials within 24 hours; some have a small workspace for scholars so they may use a collection of materials where they are housed, to save wear on both the scholar and the materials. These facilities can provide a safe and sound structure for library and archival materials but, unlike the general storage warehouse, it must be remembered that these facilities contain materials that are usually considered of permanent value. Considerable attention must be paid to the design of their environment. A number of new, flexible shelving systems are being developed for these storage facilities. However, as librarians learned in New Jersey, after the collapse of the shelves in two new facilities when they were less than half filled, careful consideration of shelving needs is essential and new materials and designs must meet those needs.[3] This must be stressed to the architect, the engineers and the construction crew.

INTERIOR DESIGN

Librarians and architects have always paid great attention to the interior space of the library building, and much has been written about the design of interior space for people. The library strives to be a welcoming place where people can be reasonably comfortable as they pursue their reading and research. Ellsworth Mason has observed, "If a library feels good to be in, it will be used."[4]

Today the planning of interior space is called environmental design, defined as "that aspect of planning the built environment which actively considers the elements of human psychology, physiology, and behavior as fundamental criteria upon which to base decisions."[5] A design consultant, working with the architect, administrator and staff, should strive to create an interior that will be attractive, comfortable and well organized to meet the needs of both the staff and the users. The plan for the interior design of the building should be an integral part of the program. In the initial phase, the consultant will offer many practical suggestions, but it is the administrator and staff who must make the ultimate decisions, as they are the people who best know the needs of their clientele.

In recent years, especially since the oil crisis that took place in the early 1970s, we have learned that people can work very comfortably in an environment where the temperature remains about 68 to 70 degrees Fahrenheit (circa 21 degrees Celsius) and the relative humidity is about 45% to 55%. Higher temperatures and relative humidity lessen comfort and efficiency. The lower the temperature and, up to a point, the relative humidity, the better it is for library and archival materials. For years, architects and librarians believed in great expanses of windows in libraries. Quite aside from the additional expense that such windows have added to the heating and cooling of a building, the light that enters through them will severely damage the materials exposed to it, and seriously compromise building security. Further, people become very uncomfortable when they are trying to work in windowed areas that become too bright and overheated or damp and gloomy.

Skylights may be attractive in public rooms, but they can and will leak. They admit unwanted light and heat on sunny days and allow too much heat to escape the building on cold days. Skylights are expensive, and they contribute neither to a repository's design for comfort nor to the preservation of its materials. Interior greenery may be attractive, but plants need more moisture than people, paper, bindings and other materials. Materials housed in greenhouses become moldy and decay very rapidly. People are not comfortable for long periods in buildings that are optimally healthful for plants. Greenery makes the control of humidity in the building difficult and costly. Careful planning, taking into consideration both the users and the materials they have come to the library to use, can lead to attractive environmental design without embellishments that benefit the decorator at the expense of comfort and common sense.

An important aspect of the interior design is safety. The architect and engineers, working with the library or archive administrator, will provide space and layouts that should meet safety codes and requirements. Attractive, durable furnishings are desired, and every year manufacturers introduce new and more wonderful, resilient, attractive materials and furnishings. Library furnishings are supposed to meet flame spread codes, such as NFPA (National Fire Protection Association) 701, which addresses the coverings and outer layers of furniture and drapery. However, there are no comprehensive standards for library furnishings. Today some furnishings do have a certain degree of fire resistance, but the materials in carpeting, upholstery and many fabrics can emit toxic fumes in a fire. Books and documents do not burn as easily as the materials in the furnishings of a building, and fires usually begin in waste baskets, carpets or furnishings, not in the book stack or archive. As we have learned from the devastating Los Angeles Public Library fires, the flash point at which flames burst out on draperies, carpeting and upholstered furniture is low. The materials in them quickly fuel the fire to an intensity that will cause spontaneous combustion. This issue has not been sufficiently addressed in the professional literature, but it is of considerable concern to the library or archive administrator. When selecting furniture, carpeting, drapery, and other furnishings for the interior of the building, be sure to inquire about the materials in the furnishings to determine how hazardous they are and under what conditions.

EXHIBITION AREA

Exhibition space is usually included in any plan for the use of interior space today. There is increased emphasis on the exhibition of library and archival materials as an important part of an institution's effort at outreach and education. There is considerable pressure to display more valued objects. However, library and archival materials are fragile and will suffer some deterioration when exhibited. Objects that are exhibited with insufficient protection will certainly be damaged; often the damage is clearly visible almost immediately. Chapter 4, "The Environment," discusses the effect that temperature, humidity and light have on library and archival materials. When exhibited, books and archival materials are exposed in a micro-environment that will often accelerate the rate of their deterioration. Only recently has the professional literature begun to deal with the topic of exhibition from the preservation perspective.

Space for the exhibition of materials in libraries and archives is being provided in more and more institutions, through renovation or during the construction of an addition or a new facility. Institutions can renovate unsatisfactory exhibition space to make it more appropriate for the objects on display. The references for this section will help in the sound planning and design of exhibition areas, and will provide some guidelines for the mounting of exhibitions so that the least amount of damage will occur to the materials on display.

NOTES

1. Ralph E. Ellsworth. *The Economics of Book Storage in College and University Libraries.* Metuchen, NJ: Association of Research Libraries and Scarecrow Press, 1969, 24.
2. "The Sliding Press of the British Museum," *The Library,* Ser. I, 3 (Oct. 1891), 414-420.
3. For information about these accidents, contact Susan G. Swartzburg at Rutgers University.
4. "A Well-Wrought Interior Design," *Library Journal,* 92:4 (Feb. 15, 1967), 743.
5. Julian Lamar Veatch, Jr. *Library Architecture and Environmental Design.* PhD. Diss. Florida State University, 1979, Introduction.

BIBLIOGRAPHY

Shelving and Storage

Boll, John J. *To Grow or Not To Grow? A Review of Alternatives to New Academic Library Buildings.* New York: Bowker, 1980. 32p. (LJ Special Report, 15)
  Reviews various book storage alternatives.

Cassatta, Mary B. "Storage of Library Material," *Encyclopedia of Library and Information Science,* vol. 29. New York: Dekker, 1980, 133-147.
  A summary article covering the issues involved in the decision to store materials outside the library.

Conger, Lucinda. "The Annex Library of Princeton University: The Development of a Compact Storage Library," *College and Research Libraries,* 31:3 (May 1970), 160-168.
  A description of the planning and operation of the library's off-site storage facility.

Creaghe, Norma S. and Douglas A. Davis. "Hard Copy Transition: An Automated Storage and Retrieval Facility for Low-Use Library Materials," *College and Research Libraries,* 47:5 (Sept. 1986), 495-499.
  Description of an automated storage/retrieval system (AS/RS) capable of storing 95,000 volumes, planned for California State University, Northridge. Books are stored in bins and there is access by computer.

Crosbie, Michael J. "Library Science: Planning for Book Conservation, Storage, and Information," *Architecture (AIA),* 79:7 (July 1990), 103-105.
  Briefly describes storage requirements for printed and electronic library collections.

Elkins, Kimball C. "President Eliot and the Storage of 'Dead' Books," *Harvard Library Bulletin,* 8:3 (Autumn, 1954), 299-312.
  Discussion of Eliot's radical idea of supplementary stacks for

infrequently used books and the opposition from both librarians and faculty. Remains topical.

Ellsworth, Ralph E. *The Economics of Book Storage in College and University Libraries.* Metuchen, NJ: Association of Research Libraries/Scarecrow Press, 1969. 135p.
　　A good discussion of the topic with information that remains useful today. Bibliography.

Gawrecki, Drahoslav. *Compact Library Shelving*, tr. Stanislav Rehak. Chicago: American Library Association, 1968. 185p. (Library Technology Publication, 14)
　　A thorough discussion from the European perspective. Bibliography.

Jeffs, Joseph E. "Saving Space, Energy and Money with Mobile Compact Shelving: Georgetown University," *Library Journal Special Report*, 1 (1976), 38-40.
　　A case study of the SpaceSaver system.

Koutz, John. "Robots in the Library: Automated Storage and Retrieval Systems," *Library Journal*, 112:20 (Dec. 1987), 67-70.
　　Summarizes traditional approaches to library storage systems and automatic storage and retrieval systems (AS/R) in industry. Preservation is a benefit of such systems as storage areas are not open to the public.

Lee, Sang Chul. *Planning and Design of Academic Library Buildings.* New York: School of Library Service, Columbia University, 1985. 449p. Illus. PhD. Diss.
　　Considerable discussion on the planning of stack areas.

Metcalf, Keyes DeWitt. "Compact Shelving," *College and Research Libraries*, 23:2 (March 1962), 103-111.
　　Advantages discussed, with methods for calculations for space needs.

Metcalf, Keyes DeWitt. "The Design of Book Stacks and the Preservation of Books," *Restorator*, 1:2 (1969), 115-125.
　　Provides a history of paper deterioration in American libraries and suggestions for changes in building design that can

curtail the damage. A review of past mistakes, present standards and unresolved problems.*

Metcalf, Keyes DeWitt. "Modular Planning and Physical Dimensions," *Planning the Academic Library*, H.F. Brown, ed. Newcastle, Eng.: Oriel Press, 1971, 33-41.
    Discussion on shelving needs.

Metcalf, Keyes DeWitt. *Planning Academic and Research Library Buildings*, 2nd ed. by Philip D. Leighton and David Weber. Chicago: American Library Association, 1986. 630p.
    This edition has considerable discussion about shelving and storage of materials; options are thoroughly reviewed. Bibliography.*

Muller, Robert H. "Economics of Compact Book Shelving," *Library Trends*, 3:2 (April 1965), 433-447.
    Reviews earlier articles on shelving and discusses varieties available in the 1960s. Of interest for those with facilities containing such shelving built in the 1950s and 1960s.

Rider, Fremont. *Compact Book Storage; Some Suggestions Toward a New Methodology for the Shelving of Less Used Research Materials*, New York: Haddam Press, 1949. 90p.
    Rider presents his ideas on book storage and use, and the method he employed at Wesleyan University, Connecticut, in the 1940s; an important early study.

Sato, Hitoshi. "Equipment and Buildings for Efficient Storage of Library Materials," *Japanese and U.S. Research Libraries at the Turning Point*. Metuchen, NJ: Scarecrow Press, 1977, 183-189.
    Discussion of storage space for books. The author believes in separation of space for storage and work, and that modular construction is unrealistic because if it is done properly, all parts of a building must be able to bear the weight of the stacks. Proceedings of the Third Japan-U.S. Conference on Libraries and Information Science in Higher Education, Kyoto, Japan, 1975.

Squillante, Alphonse M. "Specifications for Steel and Wood Stack Shelving," *Law Library Journal*, 61:2 (May 1968), 115-119.
    Discusses technical matters clearly. Provides information on

what the administrator should know and be prepared to ask about.

Ward, Alan. *A Manual of Sound Archives Administration.* Aldershot, Herts. and Brookfield, VT: Gower, 1990. 288p.
Offers detailed information on the storage of aural media.

Interior Furnishing

Balke, M. Noel. "Museum Library Facilities," *Museum Librarianship,* John C. Larson, ed. Hamden, CT: Shoestring/Library Professional Publ., 1985, 115-130.
A reasoned statement covering the equipment needs of a museum library, with the preservation of materials an important component.

Berkeley, Bernard. *Floors: Selection and Maintenance.* Chicago: American Library Association, 1968. 316p. (Library Technology Publication, 13)
A book on floors and flooring materials, covering the materials that were available at the time of publication. This book is especially valuable for information on postwar library buildings which are undergoing renovation as these floors break down. Bibliography.

Cohen, Aaron and Elaine. *Behavioral Space Planning and Practical Design for Libraries.* Croton-on-Hudson, NY: Authors, [1968]. Unpaged notebook.
A workbook prepared for a seminar given by the authors, who are professional consultants for library interior design. The information can be used in planning for preservation.

Fraley, Ruth A. and Carol Lee Anderson. *Library Space Planning.* New York: Neal-Schuman, 1989. 158p.
Provides a systematic method and practical suggestions for successful library space planning for existing facilities. The emphasis is on remodelling, with a concern for the materials reflected in its suggestions.

Hall, Richard B. "The Library Space Utilization Methodology," *Library Journal,* 103:21 (Dec. 1, 1978), 2379-2383.
Presents information in graphic form about the functional

requirements of a library; an attempt to design a tool to facilitate the planning process and lead to more effective facilities.

Irvine, Betty Jo. *Slide Libraries: A Guide for Academic Institutions and Museums,* 2nd ed. Littleton, CO: Libraries Unlimited, 1979. 321p.
Covers the physical planning and equipment of a slide library. The preservation of the collection is a concern reflected throughout the book.

"Library Furniture," *American Libraries,* 19:4 (April 1988), 261-272, 297-307.
Issue features new trends and designs in library furnishings. See especially "Working Within the System," by Gloria Novak, pp. 270-71, which provides sound information on outfitting the electronic workspace.

Mason, Ellsworth. "A Well-Wrought Interior Design," *Library Journal,* 92:4 (Feb. 15, 1967), 743-747.
Mason states, "If a library feels good to be in, it will be used." Reviews fundamentals of interior planning.*

Metcalf, Keyes D. "Equipment, Furniture and Modular Planning," *Colloquium on University Library Building.* Birmingham, Eng. and Lausanne, Switz.: Libri, 1972, 40-57. (*Libri,* Bull. Suppl. I)
Discusses suitable column spacing and column sizes that will work out well with library furniture and equipment.

Novak, Gloria, ed. *Running Out of Space—What Are the Alternatives?* Chicago: American Library Association, 1978. 160p.
Preconference on space planning held in San Francisco, June 1975. Papers cover microforms, resource sharing and cooperation, as well as new construction; case studies and discussion.*

Pierce, William S. *Furnishing the Library Interior.* New York: Dekker, 1980. 288p.
Covers the furnishing and equipping of libraries with useful information on shelving and storage.*

Tanis, Norman and Cindy Ventuleth. "Making Space: Automated Storage and Retrieval," *Wilson Library Bulletin,* 61:10 (June 1987), 25-27.

Case study of an academic library that decided to invest in an automated storage and retrieval system (AS/RS) to resolve overcrowding in the stacks. Describes how the system should work and its potential problems.

Thompson, Godfrey. "Building for Libraries," *Manual of Library Economy: A Conspectus of Professional Librarianship for Students and Practitioners*, R. Northwood Lock, ed. London: Bingley; Hamden, CT: Linnet Books, 1977, 119-134.
Discusses the interior furnishings needed in a new library building.

Veatch, Julian Lamar, Jr. *Library Architecture and Environmental Design: The Application of Selected Environmental Design Factors to the Planning of Public Library Facilities.* Tallahassee, FL: Florida State University School of Library Service, 1979. 298p. PhD. Diss.
A study of selected environmental design factors and their application to the planning of public library buildings, with emphasis on human needs. Bibliography.

Exhibition Area

Brimblecombe, Peter and Brian Ramer. "Museum Display Cases and the Exchange of Water Vapor," *Studies in Conservation*, 28:4 (Nov. 1983), 179-188.
Results of an experiment conducted which closely examined the gas exchange between the display case and the ambient air.

Casterline, Gail Farr. *Archives and Manuscripts: Exhibits.* Chicago: Society of American Archivists, 1980. 94p. (Basic Archival Series)
An excellent handbook that covers all aspects of exhibition.*

Clapp, Anne F. *Curatorial Care of Works of Art on Paper: Basic Procedures for Paper Preservation.* New York: Nick Lyons, 1987. 191p.
A sound technical reference, particularly on environmental conditions as they affect items on display.

Hinson, Karen. "Exhibitions in Libraries: A Practical Guide," *Art Documentation*, 4:1 (Spring 1985), 6-7.

A practical article on equipping exhibition space and preparing the exhibit.

Lank, Herbert. "The Function of Light in Picture Galleries," *Burlington Magazine*, 126:970 (Jan. 1984), 4-6.
Discussion of the use of artificial light, its problems and its benefits. Deterioration of materials caused by light is discussed.

O'Connor, Joan L. "Conservation of Documents in an Exhibit," *American Archivist*, 47:2 (Spring 1984), 156-163.
Discusses conservation work in preparation for an exhibit and the importance of temperature, humidity, air quality and lighting controls in the display environment.

Perkinson, Roy. "On Conservation: Problem of Lighting Works of Art on Paper," *Museum News*, 53:3 (Nov. 1974), 5-7.
The affects of light on museum objects.

Research Libraries Group. "Exhibition," *RLG Preservation Manual*. Stanford, CA: Research Libraries Group, 1986, 140-142.
Basic, clearly written instruction for the exhibition of library and archival materials. Bibliography.

Stolow, Nathan. *Conservation and Exhibitions: Packing, Transport, Storage and Environmental Conditions*. London: Butterworths, 1987. 266p. Illus. (Butterworths Series in Conservation and Museology)
A detailed manual covering all aspects of exhibition. Includes standards and guidelines as well as extensive notes.*

Stolow, Nathan. "Recent Developments in Exhibition Conservation," *Museum*, 29:4 (1979) 192-205.
A discussion of the need for conservation considerations when planning and displaying objects in an exhibition. Environmental factors are discussed; issues that need further investigation are raised.

Witteborg, Lothar P. *Good Show! A Practical Guide for Temporary Exhibitions*. Nashville, TN: American Association for State and Local History, 1981. 172p.
A guide covering advance planning, lighting, security, fabrication and installation; compiled for the Smithsonian Institution Travelling Exhibition Service.

CHAPTER 4. The Environment

INTRODUCTION

NO DOCUMENTARY MATERIAL and no library building is permanent, but both should last as long as possible. The replacement of buildings and/or the materials they house is very costly. To ensure that the materials the library or archive has collected for the benefit of its patrons last as long as possible, the building should provide a proper environment to house them. This environment will also prolong the life of the building itself.

The earliest archivists and librarians were aware of the need for a proper environment in which to house their treasures. As already discussed, this was a primary concern of archive and library administrators until the end of the last century. With the growth of the public library movement in America and its emphasis on service to people rather than to the care of collections, the need for an environment appropriate for the materials was neglected. Buildings designed to facilitate "service" were not always comfortable for people or for the collections assembled for them. Temperature, humidity, air pollution, dirt and light, working separately or in concert, cause harm to library and archival materials, just as they cause discomfort, even harm, to people.

A sound, properly built structure will provide a good home for collections. But it must be properly maintained once it is built. There are many new materials and technologies that can be used to construct sound structures and create a healthy environment within, but many can cause problems. Working with the architect and engineers to assure an appropriate environment in the library or archive requires both knowledge and concern on the part of an administrator. He or she and the staff must communicate to the architect and the contractor the necessity for a proper environment in the building. An administrator has to be aware of the appropriate standards for the protection of the materials and why it is important that they be followed.

Since the early 1970s there has been considerable interest in energy conservation. Sometimes this goes in concert with the preservation of library and archival materials; often it does not. The concern for energy savings has led to a much needed lowering of the temperature in buildings, but many institutions began to turn off all temperature controls when buildings were not used. This created a disastrous situation for museums, libraries and archives housing objects that were particularly sensitive to sudden fluctuations in temperature and humidity. Although people learned to turn off lights when they were not using them, a very good habit in the library or archive, energy conservation also led to institutional use of fluorescent rather than incandescent lighting. Fluorescent lighting, when left on over a long period of time, is cheaper to operate, but it emits a higher level of the ultraviolet rays that prove damaging to paper and other materials. Moreover, buildings that are too tightly constructed or too heavily insulated curtail the natural flow of air and thus create an atmosphere laden with pollutants and micro-organisms which is as unhealthy for people as for library and archival materials. Once again, the standards have to be very carefully reviewed with the purpose of the building in mind.

The librarian or archivist is not an architect or an engineer, but he or she can ask intelligent questions about the materials used in the construction or renovation of a building and what the specialist thinks its effects on the materials might be. If the specialist has no answer, demand it. If the environment of the building is appropriate, there will be happy and comfortable patrons, the materials will last far longer and the library/archive administrator will have demonstrated sound managerial ability.

This chapter briefly discusses the environmental problems that can plague a building and provides references for the administrator. Highly technical articles are omitted from the bibliography not only because they are of little benefit to an administrator who lacks a technical background, but also since, in many cases, new technologies will soon replace the current technology.

TEMPERATURE AND HUMIDITY

The best environment for people and for library and archival materials is a temperature range of 68 to 70 degrees Fahrenheit (21 degrees Celsius). Relative humidity (RH) should be controlled to remain relatively constant between 45% and 55%. For every degree that the temperature goes above 70 degrees Fahrenheit, the inherent destruction to books and manuscripts is increased tenfold; other materials deteriorate even more rapidly in high temperatures. Mold growth will begin to appear when the temperature and the relative humidity reach 80 degrees Fahrenheit and 80% RH; some materials will begin to show mold growth when temperature and relative humidity range in the 70s. Too low a humidity level will cause damage to materials; leather is particularly susceptible. Current investigations indicate that low temperatures and lower humidity levels (38% to 45%) prolong the life of most media housed in libraries and archives.

It is important that temperature and humidity remain relatively constant. Rapid fluctuations can do more harm to materials than a high temperature in itself. Relative humidity of more than 80% will cause mold growth regardless of the temperature, and thus is always harmful. Most materials are hygroscopic and will expand and contract with even slight variations in temperature and humidity. These contractions will break down the fabric of the object. The fluctuation will also foster the intrinsic chemical action that breaks down many materials. A fluctuation of about 10 to 12 degrees Fahrenheit in temperature and 10% to 15% humidity is acceptable, if the seasonal accommodation is done gradually. Avoiding conditions that cause rapid fluctuation can be difficult, but it is important that the HVAC (heating, ventilation, and air conditioning) system in the library, archive or museum be designed to do so.

An HVAC system that too rigidly controls the temperature and humidity level of a building throughout the year can also create serious problems. K.J. Macleod of the Canadian Conservation Institute observes, "In many buildings it is likely that an attempt to maintain a reasonable humidity in the interior during the coldest months of the year will lead to serious damage to the exterior walls of the building. This occurs because water vapour will diffuse through the wall from a region of high humidity inside to the low humidity atmosphere outside."[1] This will cause salts to form that can break down the structure of the exterior wall. Although this is more common in colder climates, it also makes it clear that when planning for a stabilized environment in the interior of a building, the exterior, or envelope, fabric of the building must be considered. The materials used to construct a repository can have a real bearing on the conditions within, and the conditions within can also have a bearing on the exterior envelope.

Although it can be expensive to design an HVAC system to maintain temperature and humidity at a fairly constant level, if this is not done, the destruction to the materials can be considerable. There have been several libraries and museums built in the past decade with such serious problems with HVAC systems that the buildings cannot be used as they were planned.

Those responsible for repositories for rare materials in a variety of media should determine the optimum storage conditions for each of the materials in the collection. Then a controlled range of temperature and humidity that is best for the collection as a whole should be established.

Very rare materials that require special storage conditions may have to be stored separately. Some repositories have cold storage vaults for materials, such as documents, photographs and films. However, materials housed in cold storage will need to be acclimated for a period of time (two to three days) before they can be used.

AIR POLLUTION

Air pollution is the enemy of both books and people. Archivists and librarians have always been aware of the serious damage that contaminated air causes to books, documents and other paper-based materials. William Blades observed this phenomenon in his classic work, *The Enemies of Books,* first published in London in 1880. London, a century ago, was particularly noxious, and Blades could not help but observe the effect on the materials in the British Museum of the chemicals in the heating and lighting materials used in the city. The effect of polluted air on people is also well-documented, although it was not until this century that librarians became more concerned with pollution's hazards to people than their materials.

Contaminating particles in the air are made up of molds, fungi, dirt, and a variety of chemicals, all of which accelerate the deterioration of all materials. Paper-based materials are particularly susceptible because of the inherent nature of paper. In order to extend the life of all library and archival materials, every effort should be made to prevent the introduction and accumulation of pollutants as well as to maintain a good level of air circulation.

In recent years there has been considerable concern about the effect of air pollution on people. Efforts have been made to clean up particularly affected areas in this country and abroad. Librarians and archivists know how difficult it is to work for any length of time in a contaminated environment. The atmosphere that is uncomfortable for users and staff is harmful to the collections. Dirt is abrasive, and the chemical component of detritus matter will react badly with the chemical composition of paper and bindings. Particulate matter is especially destructive to photographs and film, and can rapidly destroy magnetic tapes. A well-designed HVAC system will filter out particulate matter. The design of the system will depend upon the physical location of the building, the extent of its exposure to air pollution and the nature of that pollution. A well-maintained HVAC system will retard or eliminate microbiological agents.

Computers are particularly susceptible to the hazards of dust and smoke. A modern information center must be housed in a building that will protect them. Smoking and eating should never be permitted in computer areas because they can cause the loss of data. But smoke and bits of food and drink can also cause physical harm to other materials. Fortunately, a health-conscious society is creating legislation that bans smoking in public buildings, and there is more of an awareness that snacking in the library is also harmful to the materials.

A further concern is the effect that air-tight buildings, even with the most sophisticated air control and ventilation systems, have on people. It has become clear that these systems cannot provide a healthful environment. The causes of the problem are numerous; the chemicals in the materials in the construction of the building and its furnishings, and even the people themselves, emit contaminants that exceed the air system's capacity to handle them. Several citations listed in this chapter's bibliography deal with this problem, discussing the attempts to investigate its parameters. There is sufficient documentation already to indicate that the pollutants in air-tight buildings are indeed harmful to people. A careful reading of the causes will reveal that these pollutants are probably even more harmful to library and archival materials, although the extent of the damage may not be visible until someone goes to use them. Further study of this problem is called for, but it is certain that the harmful effects of air pollution on every aspect of the library and archive is one of the more serious matters that the administrator faces today. There is no question that its resolution will be costly, whether one is renovating an older facility or planning a new one.

LIGHT

The lighting of libraries and archive repositories is one of the most difficult areas to deal with when planning for a new building or for the renovation of older space. Readings on the topic are either elementary or exceedingly technical. It is important, however, to realize that "shedding light" on the topic is not impossible.

Good design of a library or archive is based not only on measurement and calculation, but also upon experience, observation, and intuition.[2] The experienced administrator will be able to integrate these qualities to ensure that the library is lit properly; is attractive, comfortable, and functional for people; and that it is protective of the materials. In addition, the cost and maintenance of the lighting is an increasingly important part of overall planning. If an administrator is aware of the problems that lighting can create, he or she will be able to work with both architect and illuminating engineer to resolve them in a satisfactory manner.

Until the invention of electrical lighting at the end of the ninteenth century, library and archive repositories were dependent upon natural light because artificial light sources were unsatisfactory. Although librarians and archivists were aware of the harm that natural light did to the materials in their care, there was no option. Even when electrical lighting was introduced, most librarians preferred natural lighting whenever possible. There is no question that people prefer to work in natural light, if that light is not too intense, and libraries are for people. Library and archival materials were, and are, secondary in too many instances. Contemporary design, until very recently, called for large windowed spaces, which are possible with the development of heating and air conditioning. Libraries still win design awards for their vast windowed spaces.[3] Ironically, these areas admit too much light, causing patron discomfort. More than one library has had to purchase drapery and ultraviolet light filters, or undertake other measures to protect people from the discomfort of intense light. The materials that have been exposed to this light are damaged almost immediately from the radiant energy that accelerates internal deterioration. Signs of this damage, such as fading, are evident within a very short period of time.

The typical lighting found in libraries and in archives is either incandescent or fluorescent. Incandescent light is more satisfactory, not only for the comfort of the reader, but also because it emits less ultraviolet radiation, that spectrum of light that is most harmful. However, as energy costs have risen, more and more institutions are using fluorescent lighting, which saves energy and is usually cheaper and easier to maintain. In a number of institutions, fluorescent lighting is now required. Only recently have architects and engineers taken a second look at fluorescent lighting and learned that it is not optimum for reader comfort. Further, it appears that fluorescent lighting may contribute to the harmful pollutants in the interior environment. Although incandescent lighting is somewhat more costly, it may prove to be far more satisfactory for primary interior lighting. Nonetheless, fluorescent lighting dominates in modern library buildings and is likely to continue to do so for some years to come. It can be shielded with special ultraviolet filters that can offer protection for up to a decade. These should be installed in all areas where materials are exposed to both fluorescent and natural lighting.

Reading about library lighting should be broad and extensive. Individuals involved in the planning of a building must look beyond the professional literature to gain an understanding of the nature of lighting, for it is the library/archive administrator who needs to keep the architect and the lighting engineer on course. Frequently, as a review of the architectural literature reveals, the architect does not realize the importance of appropriate library lighting and the desired results, both for people and for the materials. Engineers are at the other end of the spectrum, seeking the ultimate in lighting without full cognizance of the need to achieve a balance between aesthetics, function and cost, both short-term and long-term. The administrator becomes the moderator who can achieve and maintain a delicate balance which will result in library lighting that is comfortable, functional, and mindful of the collections.

The selection of readings on lighting ranges from the elementary to the technical. Although Keyes Metcalf's publications are not state-of-the-art in lighting technology, Metcalf, a practicing librarian for over seventy years, fully understood the nature of library lighting, the history of its use in libraries and that delicate balance between reader comfort, aesthetics and the preservation of library materials. Metcalf's work is a good place to begin an exploration of the topic of library lighting. Some older references are included in the bibliography, for many of the buildings planned when electric lighting was first introduced to libraries are only now being renovated, as are many newer buildings. A knowledge of how lighting was originally planned for library buildings will help resolve the problems that planners face in creating a satisfactory lighting scheme in contemporary space. In addition, some familiarity with the physics of lighting and some of its more technical aspects will facilitate communication with the architect and lighting engineer. The achievement of satisfactory library lighting is a challenge, but with a combination of technical knowledge, experience and intuition, it can be accomplished.

NOTES

1. *Relative Humidity*. Ottawa: Canadian Conservation Institute, 1978, 18.
2. *The Lighting of Buildings*. London: Faber & Faber, 1972, 19.
3. See *Library Journal*, December 1, 1985.

130

BIBLIOGRAPHY

General Reading

Abramson, Alan B. "A New Era for Building System Monitoring and Control," *Architectural Record*, 169:5 (May 1981), 118-119.
  A brief discussion of the use of micro-computers for environmental control systems.

Architect's Handbook of Energy Practice, 12 vols. Washington, DC: American Institute of Architects, 1982.
  Ten state-of-the-art monographs covering pre-design, design, and energy analysis.

Banks, Paul N. "Environmental Conditions for Storage of Paper-Based Records," *Conservation in Archives*. Paris: International Council of Archives, 1989, 77-88.
  Discusses the major elements of the environment that affect the longevity of records; paper presented at an international symposium, Ottawa, Canada, May 10-12, 1988.

Banks, Paul N. "Environmental Standards for Storage of Books and Manuscripts," *Library Journal*, 99:3 (Feb. 1, 1974), 339-343.
  Reviews the standards used in the design of the Newberry Library. Covers temperature, humidity, air cleanliness, ventilation, light, exhibition, shelving and transport, storage of microfilm, disaster control, monitoring systems. This article is most relevant for research libraries, but it gives a brief, clear statement of the factors that enter into environmental planning for all libraries.

Baynes-Cope, David. *Climate as a Factor in the Storage of Documents*. Stockholm: Kungl. Konsthogskolan, Institutet for Materialkunstap Konservatorsutbildnigne, 1977. 12p.
  A light-hearted but informative lecture on the topic of climate. It has been translated into several languages.

Braswell, Charles C. "Saving Energy in Institutional Buildings," *Heating/Piping/Air Conditioning*, 54:3 (March 1982), 54-64.
  A physical plant director at a state university describes how to establish an effective energy management system. Advocates

careful analysis of the needs of the building and stresses the effectiveness of preventive maintenance.

Bullock, Cary G., Walter E. Henry, Jr., Stanley S. Kolodkin, and Lucille Roseman. "Energy Conservation in Libraries," *Library Technology Reports,* 14:4 (July-Aug. 1978), 305-437.

Covers all aspects of energy conservation, with specific reference to preservation of collections and the special problems of rare book collections. The common-sense approach to conservation is stressed, to analyze needs and to modify as appropriate.*

Caffrey, Ronald J. "Using Energy Management Systems," *ASHRAE Journal,* 25:6 (June 1983), 33-34.

A brief introductory discussion of computerized energy management systems. Concepts are applicable to libraries. The entire issue is devoted to energy management.

Duchein, Michel. *Archives Buildings and Equipment.* Munich: Verlag Dokumentation, 1977. 201p. (ICA Handbook Series, 1)

Covers all aspects of an archive's environment, with emphasis on preservation. Bibliography. A translation of *Les Batiments et Equipements d'Archives* (Paris, 1966) with supplementary text.

Environmental Specifications for the Storage of Library and Archival Materials. Atlanta, GA: Southeast Library Network, 1985. 5p.

Clearly written and informative pamphlet that covers temperature, relative humidity, air pollution, and light. Adapted from a document prepared by the Midwest Cooperative Conservation Program.

Fisher, Thomas. "Electrifying Floors," *Progressive Architecture,* 67:2 (Feb. 1986), 116-121.

Describes wiring systems. Emphasizes the need for the architect to understand the client's needs and the integration of the electrical and HVAC systems.

Fisk, D.J. "Microprocessors and Control System Design," *Heating and Air Conditioning Journal,* 52 (Sept. 1982), 28-31.

Briefly describes how to apply direct digital control in building design.

Fisk, D.J. *Thermal Control of Buildings*. London: Applied Sciences Publishers, 1981. 246p.

Handbook covering theory and system stability; deals with the implications of digital control of systems. Technical. Selected bibliography.

Flynn, John E. and Arthur W. Segil. *Architectural Interior Systems: Lighting, Air Conditioning, Acoustics*. New York: Van Nostrand Reinhold, 1970. 306p.

Written for architects, with an emphasis on "aspects of building design that affect human sensory response and behavior." The information on air conditioning is helpful. Clearly written, with diagrams.

Gondos, Victor, Jr., ed. *Reader for Archives and Records Center Buildings*. Chicago: Society of American Archivists Committee on Archival Buildings and Equipment, 1970. 127p.

Preservation is a major consideration; covers environmental factors for buildings.

Guichen, Gael de. *Climat dans le Musee: Mesure/Climate in Museums: Measurement*. 3rd ed. Rome: International Centre for the Study of the Preservation and the Restoration of Cultural Property, 1988. 80p. French/English.

A practical handbook on the techniques and instruments used for the measurement of the museum climate.

Guldbeck, Per E. *The Care of Antiques and Historical Collections*, 2nd rev. ed. by A. Bruce MacLeish. Nashville, TN: American Association for State and Local History, 1985. 248p.

A manual on the care of historic artifacts, with advice about the housing and storage of materials under environmentally sound conditions.

Hassett, James H. "Reliable Computer Environment for Energy Savings," *Heating/Piping/Air Conditioning*, 53:4 (April 1981), 106-113.

Discussion of the potential of the computer to monitor the environment of a building; saving of energy stressed.

International Institute for the Conservation of Historic and Artistic Works. *Contributions to the London Conference on Museum Climatology*, 18-23 Sept., 1967, Garry Thomson, ed. London: Butterworths, 1968. 296p.

A collection of papers on environmental controls in museums; covers temperature, humidity, air pollution, lighting, museum design, exhibitions.

Kleinpeter, Joseph. "Computerized Maintenance," *Heating/ Piping/Air Conditioning*, 53:11 (Nov. 1981), 153-154.
Discusses the elements of computerized maintenance programs.

LaFontaine, R.H. *Environmental Norms for Canadian Museums, Art Galleries and Archives*. Ottawa: Canadian Conservation Institute, 1979. 4p. (CCI Technical Bulletin, 5) French/ English.
Requirements for temperature, relative humidity, structure, lighting, and special considerations. Drafted for directors and curators who must deal directly with architects and building engineers.

LaFontaine, R.H. *Recommended Environmental Monitors for Museums, Archives and Art Galleries*. Ottawa: Canadian Conservation Institute, 1978. 22p. (CCI Technical Bulletin, 3) French/English.
Describes instruments for monitoring environmental conditions in museums.

Lee, Sang Chul. *Planning and Design of Academic Library Buildings*. New York: Columbia University School of Library Service, 1985. 449p. Illus. PhD. Diss.
Considerable discussion on heating, ventilation, and light.

Lull, William P. *Conservation Environment: Guidelines for Libraries and Archives*, with Paul N. Banks. Albany, NY: New York State Program for the Conservation and Preservation of Library Materials, 1991. 88p.
Discusses environmental concerns, assessment, monitoring, and the establishment of practical solutions, low-cost and interim, for the improvement of the environment.*

Matthei, Robert A. "Energy Conservation and Management: A Critical Challenge for Cultural Institutions," *Technology and Conservation*, 3:1 (Spring 1978), 12-20.
Describes what cultural institutions can do to plan for energy savings without damaging collections. Discusses how to conserve energy resources.

Matthei, Robert A., ed. *Energy Management for Museums and Historical Societies.* New York: New York Hall of Science, 1982. 121p.

Focuses on energy management as it relates to maintaining appropriate museum environmental conditions. The information has been compiled from published sources and the data presented at workshops and seminars.

Merritt, Frederick S., ed. *Building Design and Construction Handbook,* 4th ed. New York: McGraw-Hill, 1982. 1479p.

A compendium of the best current building practices; several chapters deal with environmental considerations.

Meyer, William T. *Energy Economics and Building Design.* New York: McGraw-Hill, 1983. 341p.

Explains first-cost and life cycle cost implications of energy-saving design. Methods to control a building's need for energy are examined and techniques for evaluating economic implications of energy-conscious design are shown.

Motylewski, Karen. "A Matter of Control," *Museum News,* 69:2 (April 1990), 64-67.

Discussion of appropriate climate control for the protection of collections.*

Olson, Christopher. "Have Smart Buildings Flunked the Test?" *Building Design and Construction,* 27:9 (Sept. 1986), 73-74.

Brief discussion of early integrated telecommunication and building management systems that did not work.

Parker, Thomas A. "Integrated Pest Management for Libraries," *Preservation of Library Materials,* vol. 2, ed. Merrily A. Smith. Munich; New York: Saur, 1987, 103-123. (IFLA Publication, 41)

A review of the common pests found in libraries and archives. A common-sense approach to pest control is recommended. Bibliography.*

"Physical Planning Guidelines for Housing Library Systems," *Library Systems Newsletter,* 4:1 (Jan. 1984), 4-8.

A practical article stressing the necessity of housing computers in appropriate environmental conditions.

Plumbe, Wilfred J. "Climate as a Factor in the Planning of University Library Buildings," *UNESCO Bulletin for Libraries*, 17:2 (Nov.-Dec. 1963), 316-325.
An introduction to the subject.

Preservation of Historical Records. Washington, DC: National Academy Press, 1986. 108p.
Report of the Committee on Preservation of Historical Records, National Materials Advisory Board, and the Commission on Engineering and Technical Systems, National Research Council, brought together to study the methods available for the preservation of the documents housed in the National Archives. The storage of documents in an environmentally sound facility is a concern.

Shuttleworth, Riley. *Mechanical and Electrical Systems for Construction.* New York: McGraw-Hill, 1983. 742p. Illus.
A text for practitioners and students of construction on mechanical and electrical systems found in modern buildings. Covers HVAC systems, sewage and drainage, electrical systems.

Stein, Richard G. *Architecture and Energy.* Garden City, NY: Anchor Press/Doubleday, 1977. 322p.
A clearly written introduction to the problems on energy in buildings. Necessary reading for planning.*

Sterwart, G. "First Principles in Building Services Automation," *Heating and Air Conditioning Journal*, 52:3 (March 1982), 37-38.
Describes the use of electronic controls for individual plants and centralized building systems for larger buildings.

Stoecker, W.F. "Programmable Controllers," *Heating/Piping/Air Conditioning*, 53:4 (April 1981), 65-75.
Description of the computerized control of energy, using the programmable controller.

Story, Keith O. *Approaches to Pest Management in Museums.* Washington, DC: Conservation Analytical Laboratory, Smithsonian Institution, 1985. 165p.
Describes the damage that insects can cause and reviews methods of pest control, which are depending more upon maintaining an appropriate environment.

Thomson, Garry. "Specification and Logging of the Museum Environment," *International Journal of Museum Management and Curatorship*, 3:4 (Dec. 1984), 317-326.

Specifications for an appropriate museum environment. A discussion of methods for monitoring performance through the use of computerized programs.

Thumann, Albert. *Handbook of Energy Audits*, 2nd ed. Atlanta, GA: Fairmont Press, 1983. 440p.

Comprehensive practical reference on energy auditing in buildings. Covers electrical, mechanical and maintenance management.

Tisdale, Robert F. "Air Flow Controls: How Much Accuracy Can We Afford?" *Heating/Piping/Air Conditioning*, 53:8 (Aug. 1981), 57-64.

A study of the cost justification for commercial controls, with the conclusion that such controls are cost-effective.

Tollafield, Ronald. "Physical Facilities and Environmental Control," *Local Public Library Administration*, 2nd rev. ed., Ellen Altman, ed. Chicago: American Library Association, 1980, 225-240.

Good discussion on preventive maintenance; covers heating and air conditioning, energy conservation, lighting and fire prevention.

Ucar, Manas and Gail C. Doering. "Energy Conservation in Museums and Public Buildings," *ASHRAE Journal*, 24:8 (Aug. 1983), 32-37.

Report on a project to assess the energy conservation possibilities in museums with regard to their special environmental needs. The report addresses "environmental parameters which affect the preservation of collections: temperature, relative humidity, and lighting," and explains how to analyze needs.*

U.S. Department of Energy. Office of Conservation and Solar Energy. *Architects and Engineers Guide to Energy Conservation in Existing Buildings*. Washington, DC: Govt. Print. Off., 1980. 455p. (E1.26.0132/ s/n 061-000-00394-1)

Manual for architects and engineers whose work includes the analysis and modification of existing buildings to reduce both fuel consumption and operating costs.

Wessel, Carl J. "Environmental Factors Affecting the Permanence of Library Materials," Library Quarterly, 40:1 (Jan. 1970), 39-84.
A discussion of the environmental factors that cause the deterioration of library materials.

Zycherman, Lynda A. and John Richard Schrock, eds. *A Guide to Museum Pest Control*. Washington, DC: Foundation of the American Institute for Conservation/Systematics Collections, 1988. 205p.
Covers policy, law and liability; pests and pest identification; treatment. A timely guide for libraries and archives; to be used with Story, cited above. Extensive bibliography.*

Heating and Air Conditioning; Temperature and Humidity

Ackery, E.M. *Electrical Heating for Public and Commercial Libraries and Museums, Etc.* Gravesend, Eng.: Philip, 1938. 57p. (The Librarian Series of Practical Manuals, 12)
A clearly written and illustrated guide to electrical heating systems of the period. It demonstrates the concern of the profession for appropriate heating and is a useful reference for the renovation of prewar buildings.

Agnon, S. "Moisture Addition in Air Conditioning," Heating/ Piping/Air Conditioning, 53:11 (Nov. 1981), 137-141.
How best to add humidification when it is needed; deals mainly with cooling-type air conditioning apparatus.

Bromelle, N.S. "Air Conditioning and Lighting from the Point of View of Conservation," Museums Journal, 63 (1963), 32-36.
An early justification for air conditioning systems and control of lighting in museums.

Coad, William J. "Steam Heating Systems," Heating/Piping/Air Conditioning, 58:12 (Dec. 1986), 81-84,100.
Describes guidelines for the successful design of steam systems using current technology and hardware. The author notes that while such systems are not considered state-of-the-art technology, they are currently installed in about 50% of the buildings constructed in the mid-1980s. They are often the

appropriate choice for renovated facilities, and they function successfully in newly designed structures.

Dubin, Fred. "Mechanical Systems and Libraries," *Library Trends*, 36:2 (Fall 1987), 351-360.
Practical discussion of environmental factors and mechanical design, with a preservation perspective.

Faber, Oscar and J.R. Kell. *Heating and Air-Conditioning of Buildings*, 6th ed., rev. by J.R. Kell and P.L. Martin. London: Architectural Press, 1979. 645p. Illus.
A basic, clearly written text that covers all aspects of the subject; revised periodically since the first edition by Faber appeared in 1936.

Guntermann, Alfred. "Advanced Multizone Control Concepts," *Heating/Piping/Air Conditioning*, 53:11 (Nov. 1981), 80-84.
Demonstrates that desired temperatures can be maintained and energy savings are available with advanced multizone control concepts. Such systems are useful in libraries where stack areas can be maintained at lower temperatures than public areas.

Macleod, K.J. *Relative Humidity: Its Importance, Measurement and Control in Museums*. Ottawa: Canadian Conservation Institute, 1978. 14p. (CCI Technical Bulletin, 1) French/English.
Describes relative humidity (RH) and the part that it plays, in conjunction with atmospheric pollutants, in the deterioration of objects.

Mason, Ellsworth. "Air-Handling Systems in Libraries," *Mason on Library Buildings*. Metuchen, N.J.: Scarecrow Press, 1980, 39-48.
A discussion of the problems of air circulation and the systems that were available when the book was published. Updated from the article, "A Guide to the Librarian's Responsibility in Achieving Quality in Lighting and Ventilation," *Reader on the Library Building*, Englewood, CO: Microcard Edition, 1975, and in *Library Journal*, 92 (Jan. 15, 1967), 201-206.

Nordeen, Howard. "Choose the Right Thermostat to Hold Down Operating Costs," *Heating/Piping/Air Conditioning*, 54:8 (Aug. 1982), 133-140.

The emphasis is on energy conservation, but the description of the technology is useful in planning a system for a library.

Novell, B.J. "Passive Cooling Strategies," *ASHRAE Journal,* 25:12 (Dec. 1983), 23-28.
Discusses a design method, based upon average monthly temperature, to approximate needs to maintain temperature. While directed toward energy conservation, the system is also applicable to temperature control and the maintenance of consistent temperature levels.

Padfield, Timothy. "Climate Control in Libraries and Archives," *Preservation of Library Materials,* vol. 2, Merrily Smith, ed. Munich; New York: Saur, 1987, 124-138.
Describes mechanical control systems and environmental requirements for collections, with a discussion of passive climate control.*

Palmquist, Roland. *Air Conditioning: Home and Commercial.* Indianapolis, IN: Audel, 1978. 453p. Illus.
A clearly written text with practical information on the installation, operation, and servicing of air conditioning equipment. Glossary.

Quick, John. "Radiators and Natural Convectors: Two Industries Taking Different Paths," *Heating and Air Conditioning Journal,* 51:11 (Nov. 1981), 18-26.
A report on the differing attitudes toward radiators and convectors, and the developments which could bring solar heating into the central heating industry.

Sherratt, A.F.C., ed. *Air Conditioning and Energy Conservation.* New York: Nichols, 1980. 287p.
Papers cover all aspects of the topic and provide useful information for planning. Proceedings of the Conference on Air Conditioning and Energy Conservation, University of Nottingham, England, 1978.

Stolow, Nathan. *Notes on the Measurement of Relative Humidity and Temperature for Museums.* Washington, DC: American Association of Museums, 1977. 9p. (A Resource Booklet on Protection of Collections During Energy Emergencies)
How to take accurate measurements of relative humidity

(RH), prepared by the American Association of Museums Energy Workshop Planning Committee.

Thomson, Garry. *The Museum Environment*. 2nd ed. London: Butterworths, 1986. 308p. (Butterworth Series on Conservation in the Arts, Archaeology and Architecture)
    A textbook for curators and conservators that covers the effect of temperature and humidity upon collections.*

Torrance, J.S. "A Justification of Air-Conditioning in Libraries," *Journal of Librarianship*, 7:3 (July 1975), 199-206.
    An engineer's attempt to persuade library planners that an air conditioning concept is appropriate for a properly designed library and that such an installation need not be wasteful of energy.*

"Underlying Opinion," *Heating and Air Conditioning Journal*, 51:4 (April 1981), 12-13.
    Discussion of the pros and cons of underfloor heating systems.

U.S. National Bureau of Standards. *Air Quality Criteria for Storage of Paper-Based Archival Records*, prepared for the Public Buildings Service, General Services Administration and the National Archives and Records Service by Robert G. Mathey, et al. Washington, DC: Govt. Print Off., 1983. 109p.
    Recommendations based on research by the National Archives, on temperature, relative humidity and particulate matter in storage areas. Part 3.4, pp. 18-19, covers architectural factors. See also the review of the report by Norbert S. Baer in *American Archivist*, 48:1 (Winter 1985), 77-79.

Air Pollution

Baer, Norbert S. and Paul N. Banks. "Indoor Air Pollution: Effects on Cultural and Historic Materials," *International Journal of Museum Management and Curatorship*, 4:1 (March 1985), 9-20.
    Discussion of pollutants, their causes, including emissions from building materials which are introduced by heating and air conditioning systems, and their effect. Extensive bibliography.

Caruba, Alan. "An Air Quality Time Bomb Is Ticking," *Modern Office Technology,* 29:4 (April 1984), 87,90,92.
Discussion of the contaminants found in the air of modern buildings, and the physical problems experienced by staff.

Daniels, V. "Air Pollution and the Archivist," *Society of Archivists Journal,* 6:3 (April 1979), 154-156.
Discusses the pollutants that are the most troublesome to archivists and some solutions, such as protective wrappers.

Hackney, Stephen. "The Distribution of Gaseous Pollution Within Museums," *Studies in Conservation,* 29:3 (Aug. 1984), 106-116.
A discussion of pollutants in the atmosphere and their effect on different materials. References.

Indoor Air Pollution: The Complete Resource Guide. Washington, DC: Bureau of National Affairs, 1988. 2 vols.
A handbook covering all aspects of indoor air pollution including a complete survey of state indoor laws and regulations, an examination of indoor legislation and potentially important legal cases, and case studies.

McNall, Preston E. "The HVAC Engineer and Indoor Air Quality," *Heating/Piping/Air Conditioning,* 60:2 (Feb, 1988), 65-72.
Discusses the sources and the effects of pollutants, the Sick Building Syndrome (SBS), and methods of improving indoor air quality. Current standards and codes are cited.

Nero, Anthony V., Jr. "Controlling Indoor Air Pollution," *Scientific American,* 258:5 (May 1988), 42-48.
Reviews the indoor air pollutants that can be harmful to health, how they can occur, the problems involved in controlling them, and the types of regulations that might be developed to curtail the problem. The seriousness of indoor air pollution is stressed.

Rand, George. "Examining 'Sick' Buildings: Health Hazards in the Interior Environment," *Architecture,* 71:4 (Jan. 1985), 80-83.
Summary of a symposium to address the problem of indoor air pollution, jointly sponsored by the American Institute of Architects and its California chapter.

"Research and Development on Indoor Air Quality," *Energy Engineering*, 85:2 (Feb.-March 1988), 53-59.
A discussion of the American Society of Heating, Refrigerating and Air Conditioning Engineers (ASHRAE) position paper on indoor air quality. It recommends that ASHRAE standard 62: *Ventilation for Acceptable Indoor Air Quality*, be referenced by state and local building codes and that the federal government increase research.*

Sanford, E. "Air Filtration—The Unification of Standards." *Heating and Air Conditioning Journal*, 51:1 (Jan. 1981), 26-34.
Discussion of testing methods and potential problems.

Spengler, John D. and Ken Sexton. "Indoor Air Pollution: A Public Health Perspective," *Science*, 221:4605 (July 1, 1983), 9, 12-17.
Advocates an overall strategy to investigate indoor exposures, health effects, control options, and public policy alternatives.*

Sterling, Elia, Theodore Sterling and David McIntyre. "New Health Hazards in Sealed Buildings," *AIA Journal*, 72:4 (April 1983), 64-67.
A discussion of the effect that changes in building technology have caused on the indoor environment.

Thomson, Garry. "Air Pollution—A Review for Chemists," *Studies in Conservation*, 10:4 (Nov. 1965), 147-167.
Discussion of pollutants in the atmosphere and their effect upon materials. References.

U.S. National Bureau of Standards. *Air Quality Criteria for Storage of Paper-Based Archival Records*. Washington, DC: Govt. Print. Off., 1983.
See annotation above.

Wilson, Forrest. "Doctors for Sick Buildings," *Technology Review*, 89 (May-June 1986), 48-58.
Describes the new science of building diagnostics and analyzes why buildings fail. A major cause of failure is complex mechanical systems.

Light

Brill, Thomas B. *Light: Its Interaction with Art and Antiquities*. New York: Plenum, 1980. 287p.
A basic text that presumes that the reader has a modest background in general and organic chemistry. Discusses the nature of light, its properties, and its effect upon materials. Bibliography.*

"Control of Light," *Library and Archive Conservation*, George Martin Cunha and Norman Tucker, eds. Boston: Library of the Boston Athenaeum, 1972, 73-78.
A brief, clearly written statement about the effect of light on library and archival materials and measures that should be taken to curtail its damage. Paper from a seminar held in May 1971.

Fink, Jonathan S. "Lighting," *Building Design and Construction Handbook*, 4th ed. by Frederick S. Merritt. New York: McGraw-Hill, 1982, 21:1-25.
Detailed discussion of lighting and fixtures. The deleterious effect of light upon materials is not mentioned.

Fitch, James Marston. "The Control of the Luminous Environment," *Scientific American*, 219:3 (Sept. 1968), 191-202.
Provides an insight into the lighting problems faced by library and archive administrators; relates lighting to heating, cooling, and ventilation systems in consideration of the building process.*

Flynn, John E. and Arthur W. Segil. *Architectural Interior Systems: Lighting, Air Conditioning, Acoustics*. New York: Van Nostrand Reinhold, 1970. 306p. (Van Nostrand Reinhold Environmental Engineering Series)
Written for architects, with emphasis on "aspects of building design that affect human sensory response and behavior." Helpful information on lighting. Clearly written, with diagrams.

Hopkinson, Ralph Galbraith. *The Lighting of Buildings*. London: Faber and Faber, 1972. 320p.

Discusses the many considerations that go into the selection of lighting. Technical; short bibliography.*

Illuminating/Engineering Society. *Lighting of Libraries.* London: Illuminating/Engineering Society, 1966. 18p. (Technical Report, 8)
Discusses basic requirements and makes recommendations for library lighting. The correct type of lighting for specific purposes is emphasized.

Illuminating Engineering Society of North America. *IES Lighting Handbook,* 2 vols. John E. Kaufmann, ed. New York: Illuminating/Engineering Society, 1981.
Technical information on light and lighting. Bibliography.

LaFontaine, R.H. and P.A. Wood. *Fluorescent Lamps.* Ottawa: Canadian Conservation Institute, 1980. 14p. (CCI Technical Bulletin, 7) French/English
The operations and visual characteristics of fluorescent lamps are reviewed, with emphasis on choosing the correct lamp for a particular operation.

Lank, Herbert. "The Function of Light in Picture Galleries," *Burlington Magazine,* 126:970 (Jan. 1984), 4-6.
Discussion on the use of artificial light, its problems and its benefits. The deterioration of objects caused by light is noted.

Logan, H.L. "Lighting Libraries," *Library Journal,* 77:22 (Dec. 15, 1952), 2125-2129.
While the discussion of lighting is based on user needs, this article presents a rational, scientific basis for the selection of good, economical lighting for libraries. Notes that trained engineers must assist with the lighting plan.

Lull, William P. and Linda E. Merk. "Lighting for Storage of Museum Collections: Developing a System for Safekeeping of Light-Sensitive Materials," *Technology and Conservation,* 7:2 (Summer 1982), 20-25.
Provides a thorough review of lighting systems that are available for storage areas containing light-sensitive materials; case study of the illumination of a storage area in a museum.

Mason, Ellsworth. "Guide to the Librarian's Responsibility in Achieving Quality in Lighting and Ventilation," *Library Journal*, 92:2 (Jan. 15, 1967), 201-206.

Discusses intensity, light rays and glare, with some discussion of ventilation. Offers guidelines for librarians working with the architect.

Mason, Ellsworth. "Library Lighting," *Mason on Libraries*. Metuchen, NJ: Scarecrow Press, 1980, 25-38.

Discusses lighting from its visual aspect and from mechanical and technical developments in libraries. This is a revised version of an article published in several journals under varying titles.

Metcalf, Keyes DeWitt. *Library Lighting*. Washington, DC: Association of Research Libraries, 1970. 99p.

A survey and analysis of library needs with recommendations stated in non-technical terms. Remains a useful reference.*

Metcalf, Keyes DeWitt. *Planning Academic and Research Library Buildings*, rev. ed. by Philip D. Leighton and David C. Weber. Chicago: American Library Association, 1986. 631p.

Considerable discussion of library lighting and its effect on people and on materials. Much of Metcalf's sound advice in the first edition is reprinted here.

Moon, J. "Solar Loads on Shaded Windows," *Heating/Piping/Air Conditioning*, 53:12 (Dec. 1981), 63-66.

The author describes the computer program (SHADOW) that he developed to analyze the solar loads on windows with exterior shading. Although its purpose is energy conservation, it can also be applied to assess the impact of solar energy upon library materials.

Thomson, Garry. "Conservation and Museum Lighting," *Museum Information Sheet*, IS 6, 4th ed. London: Museums Association, 1985. 6p.

Although this essay deals with the problem of light on museum objects, the information provided is helpful for planning space for collection and exhibition areas.

Thomson, Garry. *The Museum Environment*. 2nd ed. London: Butterworths, 1986. 308p.

Provides extensive information on light and its effect on collections.*

"Ultraviolet Filters for Fluorescent Lamps," *CCI Notes* (Canadian Conservation Institute), 2/1 (June 1983), 1 leaf.

A brief note on problems and solutions, with a list of suppliers.

Yonemura, Gary T. *Criteria for Recommending Lighting Levels*. Washington, DC: Center for Building Technology, National Bureau of Standards, 1981. 54p. (NBSIR 8-2231)

NBS research and analysis records for developing energy and data costs, with recommendations that can be used for determining appropriate levels of illumination in an area.

CHAPTER 5. Safety, Security, Emergency Planning, and Insurance

INTRODUCTION

SAFETY AND SECURITY, for the sake of the patrons, the staff and the materials, are important factors in the planning of library and archival facilities. Over the past twenty years, library and archive managers have become more aware of the need for careful planning for safety and security, prodded not a little by government regulations and also by the very real threats to public institutions that accelerated in the 1970s.

Safety and security expert John Morris writes, "Building security can be promoted by the physical design and layout of the building itself, through detection devices that ward off or warn of intruders, and through inexpensive commonsense measures."[1] When construction is anticipated, whether for a new building, an addition to the original structure, or a renovation, the time to plan for safety and security begins with the preparation of the program. The approach that the library will take should be thought through before the architect enters the picture. The architect, working with the security consultant, can bring these plans to fruition in a successful way that will meet the needs of a library or archive.

Planning for emergencies should also be done when planning new facilities. This is especially important if the building will undergo renovation or if an addition is to be constructed. An emergency plan will help an institution focus on its needs for the protection of collections and the people who use them. Insurance coverage is an important, though frequently neglected, component of planning for safety, security and emergencies. Morris writes, "The insurance needs of libraries vary according to the size of the library and the nature of the collections. These needs are also affected by the design and construction of the building, and the level of protection it offers against various perils."[2] The planning phase of a new building, an addition or renovation provides the opportunity for the administrator to take a hard look at the matter of insurance coverage, both for the duration of construction and for the collection once the structure is open and operating. An experienced commercial insurer's advice can be invaluable in planning a building that will offer maximum safety and minimum insurance costs.

This chapter's bibliography provides selected readings on safety, security, emergency planning, fire safety, and insurance. Although the emphasis of this book is on the preservation of the materials in the collections, the safety and security of the people who use the facility and the materials in it cannot be considered separately. What is safe for people is also safe for the collections.

LIBRARY SECURITY

With the well-publicized increase in the number of thefts and crimes committed in or against libraries, librarians and archivists are finding it necessary to analyze and reevaluate their current security policies and procedures. The rise in the cost of books, periodicals and other library materials, and the high degree of inconvenience to patrons and staff when materials are found missing or damaged, have made security a priority for the administrator. For the archive administrator or the rare book curator, the problem of theft and mutilation of materials is of even greater concern, since the materials lost or damaged are rare or unique and usually irreplaceable.

In his book, *Design for Security*, Richard J. Healy writes, "Physical security controls are an essential factor in protecting modern facilities."[3] Librarians and archivists have learned that it is necessary to have physical controls to protect collections; although people are essential to the security system, they are no longer sufficient protection against theft and mutilation of collections. The first step in planning an integrated security system for a library or archive is to carefully and completely analyze security and fire protection needs and requirements. This should be done in the planning stage when constructing a new building or renovating an older structure. Healy writes, "Consideration must be given to the security of utilities in the site layout plan. All main control valves, regulators, switches, power controls, and so on, that are vital to the continued operation of the facility should be located within the security-controlled interior of the facility and be adequately protected against tampering, vandalism and sabotage."[4] The placement, or siting, of a structure, its entrances and exits, all have an impact on the ability to maintain a secure building.

The security industry is more than willing to cooperate with libraries and archives to help develop adequate security measures that will meet the needs of a repository. Here, also, a consultant can be brought in to make an initial survey of institution's needs. This consultant will work closely with the planning team to see that these needs are met in the final structure. The industry is constantly developing new and better security systems, and the library or archive manager, even if not planning construction in the immediate future, should stay abreast of these developments by following the literature.

The Rare Book and Manuscript Section (RBMS) of the American Library Association, working in close cooperation with the Society of American Archivists (SAA) and the Antiquarian Booksellers Association of America (ABAA), has formed the Security Committee to study ways to deal with theft or premeditated damage to library and archival materials. The committee is developing guidelines and model legislation to help curtail theft and to provide for collection security. The work of the concerned professional associations should be followed closely in the literature. Facility planners may want to attend meetings of the RBMS Security Committee at the

American Library Association annual conferences to take advantage of its collective expertise. The members of this committee, and others working closely with it, are an invaluable resource in planning for security in new or renovated space.

The bibliography on security provides references on the problem of dealing with the financial burden of increased security, descriptions of electronic and non-electronic security equipment and techniques, as well as the architecture of the library or archive and crime prevention. The bibliography is selective. Because the topic is a critical one, the administrator is well advised to turn to a broader spectrum of material that is available, including readings on specific security measures and equipment. Security is an important matter, both for the preservation of the materials in our repositories and for the safety of the individuals who use and work with them.

EMERGENCY PLANNING

Planning for an emergency is a primary management responsibility of library and archival administrators, yet it is rarely done prior to an emergency. Administrators and staff believe that "it can't happen here" and put off the task of planning in order to meet the more immediate needs of the institution. However, an emergency can strike suddenly, and with devastating impact. The four elements, earth, air, fire and water, separately or in combination, can wreak havoc upon a library, archive or museum and its collections. No matter where a repository is located, it is subject to the elements. Architect Ian Davis has observed that the best time "to instigate major mitigation measures to offset the risk of disasters . . . is following some catastrophe. It is perhaps only at this time that officials are sufficiently persuaded by public opinion to consider long-term needs which are usually completely overwhelmed by short-term expediency. Therefore some of the most significant innovations in disaster mitigation have occured in the aftermath of earthquakes, floods, etc."[5] This, however, is an unfortunate time to do so.

The *ideal* time to work toward the prevention of emergency situations is in the planning phase of a building or renovation, not after disaster has struck. The best protection against an emergency or a disaster, be it of natural or man-made causes, is prevention. Fire prevention consultant John Morris writes, "Every library, without exception, should have at least a rudimentary fire and water disaster plan, commencing with simple routines for the fire emergency."[6]

There are six objectives of emergency planning which should be a part of the preparation of the program for a new building, addition, or renovation:

1. to lessen the potential for loss by anticipating the possibilities and appropriately reducing them whenever possible;
2. to ensure that public and private agencies who understand the nature of an institution's collections and its priorities will be called in during an emergency;
3. to establish normal conditions promptly and efficiently after an emergency;
4. to lessen the chances of recurrence by taking advantage of experience gained;
5. to ensure that adequate orientation and training have been given the staff, and that this training is updated on a continuing basis; and
6. to ensure frequent inspection by appropriate agencies in order to prevent changed conditions from having a deleterious effect upon the safety and security of the building.

An institution should have one staff member, who is designated the emergency planning officer, responsible for the safety and security of both people and materials. That individual should work closely with, or be a part of, the planning team from the beginning of the planning phase. It is hoped that an institution will have an emergency plan in place prior to developing plans for a new or renovated facility. If not, the preparation of such a plan is essential prior to construction, while the program is being prepared. The emergency planning officer is usually responsible for the institution's program for fire prevention, the maintenance of fire protection equipment and services, safety and security, insurance coverage, the maintenance of the physical plant, staff training and public relations relating to emergency planning as well as at the time of an emergency. In some institutions, emergency planning is a part of the preservation officer's responsibilities, as it is an important component of a preservation program. Many institutions have health and safety committees; their input can be critical in the planning process.

If the library or archive is to be renovated or if an addition is to be built, planning for emergency becomes even more important. Not only is this the appropriate time to take measures to protect against future emergencies; it will allow the realistic manager to take notice of hazards that arise during construction. Library and archival literature is filled with case studies of disasters that occurred in operating libraries during construction.

Specialists in disaster planning and salvage, including George M. Cunha, Hilda Bohem, and Toby Murray, recommend that an institution form a *Disaster Recovery Action Team* (DRAT—the Oklahoma statewide team is known as ODRAT) made up of calm, quick-witted staff members, with the calmest and quickest appointed director. This individual has the responsibility to keep thoroughly informed and up-to-date in disaster recovery techniques. He or she should be a part of the planning team, since he or she will have responsibility for salvage operations in the facility should disaster strike. Murray suggests that "the team leader be a member of the administrative staff, because then he/she will have ready access to the money needed for salaries, supplies, services, etc. and will be better able to communicate with the administration and the media."[7] It is essential that the team leader be completely familiar with the building.

When an emergency plan is prepared, a building must be carefully surveyed to identify potential hazards. This can be done during the planning process for a new building and should be done when a building is to be renovated or to have an addition built—even if the institution already has an emergency plan. Components of a survey include the building's history, its design, heating plant, electrical system, plumbing, the placement of concealed spaces, the placement of windows, the roof and the interior furnishings. Lighting, exits and fire protection equipment are all important components of the plan for a new or remodeled facility and also for the emergency plan.

There are now a number of excellent articles and books available that deal with emergency planning, and many institutions have made their own emergency plans available to others. The literature should be reviewed, and a number of individual plans studied, to determine the approach that is best suited for each institution. In addition, a number of states, such as Illinois, Oklahoma, and New York, have developed, or are developing, statewide emergency and disaster plans. These plans were developed through their state library agencies which serve as the source of information and advice.

FIRE PROTECTION

Fire protection is an important element in the planning for any structure, especially for libraries and archives that are filled with valuable and often irreplaceable materials. A natural disaster, an accident, or carelessness can bring fire in its wake. Following the fire comes the water, which can be even more devastating to library and archival materials. Many institutions, states, or localities will have regulations regarding fire safety. However, a knowledge of library and archival materials and of their adverse reaction to these elements will be helpful in planning for fire safety in a building. There is now considerable literature on the subject for libraries and archives. The publications of the National Fire Protection Association (NFPA) in Boston, Massachusetts, will prove especially helpful in the planning process. The administrator should be familiar with the literature of fire safety in library and archives and be able to work with the architect to develop methods of curtailing its effect on collections.

INSURANCE

Insurance policies vary widely for library and archive repositories and their collections. It is important that an administrator be cognizant of the extent and the limits of coverage when a construction project is planned. This may be the time to rethink an institution's approach to insurance. Several companies are now sensitive to the special needs of libraries, archives and museums. They understand the need to respond promptly when there is an emergency situation and provide policies that offer adequate coverage for documentary materials. The readings cited are selected to give an administrator a perspective from which to review the issue of insurance.

NOTES

1. *The Library Disaster Preparedness Handbook.* Chicago: American Library Association, 1986, 75.
2. *Ibid.*, 94.
3. 2nd ed., NY: Wiley, 1983, 2.
4. *Ibid.*, 136.
5. "Appropriate Technology: The Modification of Unsafe Housing Following Disasters," *Architectural Digest*, 49:7 (July 1979), 193.
6. "Is Your Library Safe From Fire?" *Library and Archives Security*, 3:3/4 (1980), 145.
7. Correspondence, November 1986.

BIBLIOGRAPHY

General

Metcalf, Keyes DeWitt. *Planning Academic and Research Library Buildings*, 2nd ed. by Philip D. Leighton and David C. Weber. Chicago: American Library Association, 1986. 630p.

Contains considerable information, theoretical and practical, about planning buildings for safety, security and protection against disasters.

Morris, John. *The Library Disaster Preparedness Handbook*. Chicago: American Library Association, 1986. 142p.

A comprehensive review of preventive measures for libraries of all sizes, with a chapter on designing library buildings. Covers basic building security, problem patrons, theft and mutilation, fire protection, water damage, insurance and risk management.

Strassberg, Richard. *Conservation, Safety, Security, and Disaster Considerations in Designing New or Renovated Library Facilities at Cornell University Libraries*. Ithaca, NY: Cornell University Libraries, 1984. 10p.

A document prepared for Cornell's needs, but will serve as a useful planning document for all libraries.*

Toronto Area Archivists Group. *An Ounce of Prevention: A Handbook on Disaster Contingency Planning for Archives, Libraries and Records Centres*, John P. Barton and Johanna G. Wellheiser, eds. Toronto: Toronto Area Archivists Group Education Foundation, 1986. 191p.

Covers all aspects of planning for and coping with disaster. It contains considerable information that can be used in the planning process for new facilities. Topics covered include the building code, fire detection and extinguishing systems, security systems, occupational health and safety, storage, fumigation and pest control, insurance and the rehabilitation of materials. Proceedings of a Symposium on Disaster Contingency Planning for Information Managers in Archives, Libraries and Record Centres, Toronto, 1985.*

Security

Armstrong, Norma. "Essentials of Library Security: the Librarian's View," *SLA News,* 144 (March-April, 1978), 43-47.
Covers security measures that may be taken to safeguard library resources. Deals with such issues as external security, internal security, deterrents and safeguards, security systems, surveillance, precision scales and insurance coverage.

Association of Research Libraries. Office of Management Studies. *Collection Security in ARL Libraries.* Washington, DC: Association of Research Libraries, 1984. 94p. (SPEC Kit 100)
Includes two questionnaire forms, ten policies and procedures documents and two task force reports, plus a selective bibliography.

Bahr, Alice Harrison. *Book Theft and Library Security Systems, 1981-82.* White Plains, NY: Knowledge Industry Publ., 1981. 157p.
An update of the 1978 edition. Discusses problems of theft and security. Includes a chapter on "Measuring Book Loss," and a review of electronic and other security systems.

Behrends, Jeannette D. "Security Conscious Site Design," *Progressive Architecture,* 68:3 (March 1987), 140-142.
Emphasizes the need for security planning from the time that a site is selected.

Bommer, Michael and Bernard Ford. "A Cost-Benefit Analysis for Determining the Value of an Electronic Security System," *College and Research Libraries,* 35:4 (July 1974), 270-279.
Methods and results of a study by the Van Pelt Library, University of Pennsylvania, to estimate document loss as a result of theft.

Bose, Keith. *Video Security Systems,* 2nd ed. London: Butterworths, 1982. 224p.
Sourcebook on the security applications of closed circuit television (CCTV). Describes how to procure and maintain a video security system, with tips on installation and maintenance.

Bostick, William A. *The Guarding of Cultural Property.* Paris: UNESCO, 1977. 40p. (Protection of the Cultural Heritage. Technical Handbooks for Museums and Monuments)
   Thorough introduction to security needs. Bibliography.

Brand, Marvine. "Security of Academic Library Buildings," *Library and Archival Security*, 3:1 (Spring 1980), 39-47.
   Discusses the physical and operational security of academic library buildings. Provides a basic awareness checklist. Based on a security study done at the University of Houston.

Clamen, Michel. "Museums and the Theft of Works of Art," *Museum*, 26:1 (1974), 10-19.
   Examines the problem and its causes; offers suggestions to curtail theft.

Fennelly, Lawrence. *Museum, Archive and Library Security.* Woburn, MA: Butterworths, 1983. 912p.
   Contributions from security professionals at a variety of institutions. Offers practical information covering all aspects of security fundamentals: insurance, security management, fire protection and emergency planning, physical security controls, utilizing the guard force and investigating theft. Extensive bibliography by John E. Hunter.*

Guldbeck, Per E. "Planning Security for Building and Collections," *Care of Antiques and Historical Collections*, 2nd rev. ed. by A. Bruce MacLeish. Nashville, TN: American Association for State and Local History, 1985, 42-50.
   Information on built-in security measures for collections.

Hanff, Peter. "Library Theft Protection," *College and Research Libraries News*, 45:6 (June 1984), 289-90.
   Report on the results of the Rare Books and Manuscripts Section Security Committee's informal survey of collection security precautions among North American libraries.

Healy, Richard J. *Design for Security*, 2nd ed. New York: Wiley, 1983. 280p. Illus.
   Written for security personnel, architects, planners and managers; emphasizes security as a key management function.

Its purpose is "to demonstrate how the use of proper planning and design, as well as of modern techniques and devices, can significantly reduce costs and at the same time improve the protection program."

Hopf, Peter S., ed. *Handbook of Building Security Planning and Design.* New York: McGraw-Hill, 1979. Separate pagination by chapter.

A clearly written and practical handbook for architects. Sections cover such topics as design considerations, security from natural disasters, security components. Chapter 28: "Libraries," by Raymond M. Holt, pp. 28:1-20, discusses security requirements in all types of libraries.

International Committee on Museum Security. *Museum Security Survey*, based on the document by George H.H. Schroeder; Diana Menkes, ed.; Marthe de Moltke, transl. Paris: International Council of Museums, 1981. 116p.

A companion volume to *Museum Security*, by Robert Tillotson (see following). The survey was in the form of questionnaires, each section relating to an aspect of museum security. Includes risk assessment and analysis, museum surroundings, building, collections, responsibilities, internal and fire security and protection against incidents. Many of the questions are of relevance to libraries and archives.

Jones, Barclay, ed. *Protecting Historic Architecture and Museum Collections from Natural Disasters.* London: Butterworths, 1986. 400p.

Handbook on the destructive aspects of earthquakes and other natural disasters, preventive measures, mitigation of loss, emergency and rescue activities.

Keck, Caroline K., Huntington T. Block, Joseph Chapman, John B. Lawton, and Nathan Stolow. *A Primer on Museum Security.* Cooperstown, NY: New York State Historical Association, 1966. 85p.

Chapters cover physical security, insurance, environmental security and lighting. Bibliography.

Keck, Caroline K. "Security Depends on People," *Curator* (American Museum of Natural History), 10:1 (March 1967), 54-59.

Discusses the training and role of the conservator in the security program.

Kleberg, John R. "Rx for Library Security," *Library and Archival Security*, 4:4 (1982), 23-30.
Discusses the need for coordination between librarians and security professionals to develop a library security program; covers communication, survey inventory, program design and implementation.

Lincoln, Alan Jay. *Crime in the Library: A Study of Patterns, Impact and Security.* New York: Bowker, 1984. 179p.
Covers theft, vandalism, robberies and assault, problem patron behavior; an interdisciplinary approach to help the reader understand the issues and take steps to minimize the effects. Tables and checklists on crime categories, frequencies and state and national problems. Includes a security checklist.

Lincoln, Alan Jay, ed. "Protecting the Library," *Library Trends*, 33:1 (Summer 1984). Entire issue.
Contains a series of essays that examine the issues related to the protection of the library, its contents and its users.*

Lucker, E. "Theft Prevention in the Library," *Open*, 13:1 (Jan. 1981), 8-13.
Considers both electronic security systems and alternatives to security systems as methods of theft prevention.

Matthews, Joseph R. "Security and Automated Library Systems: A Ticking Time Bomb," *Information Technology and Libraries*, 2:3 (September 1983), 265-271.
Covers security of computer systems by providing an analysis of four categories (physical security, access control, hardware and software security, personnel security) through which security can be improved. Includes an Automated Library System Security Checklist.

Newman, Oscar. *Architectural Design for Crime Prevention.* Washington, DC: National Institute of Law Enforcement and Criminal Justice, March 1978. 214p.
Deals with the design of urban residential areas, not public buildings, but some design considerations can be applied.

Pegg, M.A. "Security Systems in Open-Access Libraries," *Liber Bulletin*, 16 (1981), 49-54.

Discusses new problems in library architecture, specifically security measures in open-access libraries.

Sable, Martin H. "The Protection of the Library and Archive: An International Bibliography," *Library and Archival Security*, 5:2/3 (Summer/Fall 1983). 183p. Special issue.

Bibliography that is international in scope and fairly complete. Arranged chronologically by topic, without annotation. Covers theft and security.

Schnabolk, Charles. *Physical Security: Practices and Technology.* Woburn, MA: Butterworths, 1983. 416p.

Includes information on every aspect of physical security, with information on the latest developments in the intrusion detection field.

Smith, Frederick E. "Supplementary Deterrents in Library Security," *Library and Archival Security*, 6:1 (Spring 1984), 49-56.

Discusses practical supplements to an electronic security system, such as window screens, exit control, protected housing for current periodicals, and user education.

Sutcliffe, Charles. "A Model for the Financial Appraisal of Electronic Book Security Systems with an Application to Berkshire County Libraries," *Library and Archival Security*, 6:4 (Winter 1984), 27-42.

A model for the appraisal of book security systems.

Tillotson, Robert F. *Museum Security*, Diana D. Menkes, ed.; Marthe de Moltke, transl. Paris: International Council of Museums, 1977. 244p. English/French

Discusses some sophisticated security equipment and techniques, and includes a chapter on architectural planning. Much of the material in this volume is applicable to libraries and archives.

Traister, Daniel, "Book Theft is Focus of Two-Day Conference," *AB Bookman's Weekly*, 72:16 (Oct. 17, 1983), 2443-2446.

A report on the Oberlin College Conference of librarians, booksellers, lawyers and law enforcement personnel who met to examine their mutual concern about book theft, and their desire to develop a unified approach in arriving at preventive measures to combat the problem.

Walch, Timothy. *Archives and Manuscripts: Security.* Chicago: Society of American Archivists, 1977. 30p. (Basic Manual Series)
Covers planning, staffing, methods of deterrent and the legal aspects of archival security. Bibliography.

Watstein, Sarah Barbara. "Book Mutilation: An Unwelcome By-product of Electronic Security Systems," *Library and Archival Security,* 5:1 (Spring 1983), 11-33.
Reviews the available electronic security systems and presents the results of a survey of the libraries represented on the Research Libraries Group (RLG) Preservation Committee. The author urges further investigation of this problem and a study of the costs.

Weber, Thad L. *Alarm Systems and Theft Protection.* Woburn, MA: Butterworths, 1978. 385p.
Explains in non-technical terms the broad range of security systems that are available.

Emergency Planning

Bohem, Hilda. *Disaster Prevention and Disaster Preparedness.* Los Angeles: University of California, 1978. 23p.
Provides an outline for a disaster preparedness plan and a disaster prevention checklist. Report of the University of California Task Group on the Preservation of Library Materials; a useful model, especially for larger library systems.

Buchanan, Sally A. *Disaster Planning, Preparedness and Recovery for Libraries and Archives.* Paris: UNESCO, 1988. (RAMP Study)
Manual with guidelines for planning for disaster and recovery, including sample building survey forms and a 24-page bibliography by Toby Murray.

Building Practices for Disaster Mitigation, Richard Wright, Samuel Kramer and Charles Culver, eds. Washington, DC: U.S. National Bureau of Standards, 1973. 474p.
Presents recommendations for planning and construction to

curtail the consequences of natural disasters. Technical papers; bibliography. Proceedings of the National Workshop on Building Practices for Disaster Mitigation, Boulder, Colorado, 1972.

Campbell, Robert P. "Disaster Recovery: A Game Plan," *Security Systems Administration*, 12:3 (March 1983), 16-19.
    Emergency planning and disaster recovery for computer facilities.

Canadian Conservation Institute. "Planning for Disaster Management," *CCI Notes*, 14/1-3 (May 1988). 8p.
    Covers planning and hazard analysis; basic checklist.

Eulenberg, Julia Niebuhr. *Handbook for the Recovery of Water Damaged Business Records*. Prairie Village, KS: ARMA International, 1986. 55p.
    Disaster recovery guidelines covering the spectrum of records, including paper, magnetic media and micrographics.

Fortson-Jones, Judith. "How to Develop a Disaster Plan for Book and Records Repositories," *History News*, 38:5 (May 1983), 30-31.
    A brief, practical and informative article outlining the basics for planning.

Langelier, Gilles and Sandra Wright. "Contingency Planning for Cartographic Archives," *Archivaria*, 13 (Winter 1981/82), 47-58.
    Excellent discussion of emergency planning in general, followed by an account of the contingency planning in the National Map Collection, Public Archives of Canada.

Metropolitan Reference and Research Library Agency. *Hell and High Water*, Barbara J. Rhodes, comp. New York: METRO, 1988. 55p. (METRO Misc. Publ. 35)
    Text provides basic information on preservation planning. Compiled for a series of workshops on disaster planning and coping; the resource notebook is comprehensive.

National Disaster Resource Referral Service. *A Selected, Annotated Bibliography on Emergency Planning and Management*. Arlington, VA: National Disaster Resource Referral Service, 1984. 6p.
    An annotated bibliography prepared for individuals responsible for emergency response.

O'Connell, Mildred. "Disaster Planning: Writing and Implementing Plans for Collection-Holding Institutions," *Technology and Conservation*, 8:2 (Summer 1983), 18-24.
   Covers planning for an emergency, collection surveys, salvage.

O'Connell, Mildred. "Disaster Planning for Libraries," *AB Bookman's Weekly*, 71:25 (June 20, 1983), 4693-4701.
   A general essay on disaster planning with many practical tips, written by a specialist from the Northeast Document Conservation Center, a regional center for the conservation of library and archival materials that specializes in disaster assistance.

Solley, Thomas T., Joan Williams and Linda Baden. *Planning for Emergencies: A Guide for Museums*. Washington, DC: Association of Art Museum Directors, 1987. 72p.
   Provides a framework for a museum to meet its own needs. Covers disaster planning, prevention and response. Bibliography.

Spawn, Willman. "Disasters: Can We Plan for Them? If Not, How Can We Proceed?" *A Manual of Archival Techniques*. Harrisburg, PA: Historical and Museum Commission, 1979, 71-76; reprinted in *Preservation of Library Materials*, Joyce R. Russell, ed. New York: Special Libraries Association, 1980, 24-29.
   A basic article that provides step-by-step advice for planning and salvage.

Stanford University Libraries. *Disasters, Preservation and Coping*, James N. Myers and Denise D. Bedford, eds. Stanford, CA: Stanford University Libraries, 1981. 177p.
   Proceedings of a conference for librarians on emergency planning and salvage held at Stanford in 1980. It includes an analysis of the Stanford Library disaster, some sound general information, and an excellent introduction by Stanford's librarian, David Weber.

U.S. National Weather Service. *Earthquake History of the United States*. Washington, DC: Government Printing Office, 1973. 208p.
   History of prominent earthquakes through 1970, documented

with earthquake data, listed and described by region and state. Glossary of terms.

Upton, M.S. and C. Pearson. *Disaster Planning and Emergency Treatments in Museums, Art Galleries, Libraries, Archives and Allied Institutions.* Canberra, Australia: Institute for the Conservation of Cultural Material, Inc., 1978. 54p.
A manual for all cultural institutions. It offers recommendations for organizing emergency services, discusses the technical expertise that might be needed and offers advice on the treatment of damaged materials.

Waters, Peter. *Procedures for Salvage of Water-Damaged Library Materials.* 2nd ed. Washington, DC: Library of Congress, 1978. 30p.
A guide to reclaiming water-damaged library and archival materials, including assessment of damage, freezing, salvage team work, cleaning, and drying without freezing. This pamphlet belongs in every library.*

Selected Emergency Plans

Anderson, Hazel and John E. MacIntyre. *Planning Manual for Disaster Control in Scottish Libraries and Record Offices.* Edinburgh: National Library of Scotland, 1985. 75p.
A "blueprint" to be used in the preparation of disaster control plans with a minimum outlay of staff time. Covers prevention, insurance, reaction procedures. Its use is not limited to Scottish institutions.

Association of Research Libraries. Office of Management Studies. *Preparing for Emergencies and Disasters.* Washington, DC: 1980. 109p. (SPEC Kit 69)
Includes selections from the manuals of selected libraries covering disaster preparedness, protecting people and property, salvaging library materials. Three case histories.

Cornell University Libraries. *Emergency Manual.* Ithaca, NY: Cornell University Libraries, 1976. 42p.
A manual that can serve as a model for a variety of institutions.

Fortson-Jones, Judith. *Manual for Records Preservation and Disaster Planning for State Government Agencies in Nebraska* (20p.); *A Manual for Paper Preservation and Disaster Planning for Archives, Libraries and Museums in Nebraska* (20p.); *A Manual for Records Preservation and Disaster Planning for Local Government Agencies in Nebraska* (20p.) Lincoln, NE: Nebraska State Historical Society, 1981.
   Three basic manuals prepared for state agencies.

Harvard University Library. Subcommittee on Emergency Procedures. *Emergency Guidelines for Harvard Libraries.* Cambridge, MA: 1982. Unpaged.
   Instructions for fire and evacuation, flooding and water leaks. Includes instruction forms and contact people.

New York University Libraries. Preservation Committee. *Disaster Plan Workbook.* New York: New York University Libraries, 1984. Unpaged.
   A fill-in-the-blanks notebook, originally prepared for the New York University Libraries but adaptable to many library and archive situations.

Fire Protection

Bierwirth, Ed. "When Retrofitting Build in the Degree of Fire Protection Needed," *ASHRAE Journal*, 26:4 (April 1984), 48-49.
   Discusses how to analyze a building and work with a consultant; especially useful for libraries adding more mechanical and electrical facilities.

Clarke, F.B. and D.W. Raisher. *Attacking the Fire Problem: A Plan for Action.* Washington, DC: National Bureau of Standards, 1976. 34p. (NBS Publ. 416)
   Objectives of the Center for Fire Research, Institute of Applied Technology, National Bureau of Standards.

Colburn, Robert E. *Fire Protection and Suppression.* New York: McGraw-Hill, 1975. 342p.
   Text that presents basic information on the field of fire technology.

Ferguson, David J. "Designing for Fire and Life Safety: The Development of Suitable Systems for an Underground Museum," *Technology and Conservation,* 7:4 (Winter, 1982), 26-30.

A description of the system developed for the underground addition to the Smithsonian Institution. The plan included fire prevention; an automatic sprinkler system was installed; Halon 1301 is in the special collection vaults.

Fielding, George H., F.J. Woods and H.E. Johnson. "Halon 1301: Mechanism of Failure to Extinguish Deep-Seated Fires," *Journal of Fire and Flammability,* 6 (Jan. 1975), 37-43.

Warns that Halon 1301 may fail to completely extinguish fire originating in a mass of porous or stacked cellulose materials; discusses its potential danger to humans.

Fortson-Jones, Judith. "Fire Protection for Libraries," *Catholic Library World,* 53:5 (Dec. 1981), 211-213.

Discusses several fire protection systems, including wet and dry sprinkler systems, high expansion foam, carbon dioxide and Halon.

Hammack, James M. "Talking Extinguishing Equipment: the Halons," *Fire Journal,* 64:3 (May 1970), 60-62. (NFPA Reprint FJ70-27)

A history of the use of halogenated hydrocarbons (halons) as fire extinguishants and the status of modern halons, especially Halon 1301 (bromotrifluoromethane) in fire protection.

Harvey, Bruce K. "Fire Hazards in Libraries," *Library Security Newsletter,* 1:1-4 (1975), 6-7; 1,4-5; 9-10; 1,5.

Examines fire protection equipment that should be considered when designing a new library; suppressant systems and sprinklers; installation of systems in existing libraries; working with the Fire Department and salvage of damaged materials.*

Lie, T.T. *Fire and Buildings.* Barking, Eng.: Applied Science, 1972. 276p. (Architectural Science Series)

Deals with various aspects of protection against spread of fire and collapse in buildings. Emphasizes the prevention of the spread of fire by the compartmentalization of a building with fire-resisting construction. Consideration is given to experimental and theoretical methods of determining the fire resistance of structural elements such as floors, wood columns and beams.

Morris, John. "Fire Protection in the Library," *Construction Specifier*, 42:10 (Oct. 1989), 133-141.

Covers the history of fires and policies of fire protection; bookstack construction and its effect on the spread of fire; types of automatic suppressant systems and descriptions of buildings where they are installed.*

Morris, John. "Is Your Library Safe From Fire?" *Library and Archival Security*, 3:3/4 (Fall/Winter 1980), 139-145.

Suggestions for strengthening a library against arson or fire, with information about sprinkler systems.

Morris, John and Irvin D. Nichols. *Managing the Library Fire Risk*, 2nd ed. Berkeley: University of California, 1979. 147p.

Provides information relating to fire risk for libraries and means of protection against loss from fire, with emphasis on automatic systems of protection. This information was originally assembled for the University of California library system.

National Fire Protection Association. *Designing Buildings for Fire Safety*. Boston, MA: NFPA, 1975. 125p.

A compilation of 23 articles from *Fire Journal* and *Fire Technology*. Covers good fire-safe building design.

National Fire Protection Association. *Fire Protection Guide on Hazardous Materials*. 9th ed. Boston, MA, NFPA, 1986. 251p.

Information on the hazardous properties of chemicals. Includes flashpoint index of trade name liquids; fire hazard properties of flammable liquids, gasses and volatile solids; hazardous chemical data; manual of hazardous chemical reactions; and a recommended system for the identification of the fire hazard of materials. Revised regularly.

National Fire Protection Association. *Protection of Libraries and Library Collections*. Boston, MA: NFPA, 1985. 24p. (NFPA Publ. 910)

Recommended practice for the protection of library collections from fire. Updated frequently.*

National Fire Protection Association. *Sprinkler Systems Standard and Handbook*, rev. ed. Quincy, MA: NFPA, 1989. 500p.

A text for people who design, install and inspect automatic sprinkler systems; provides technical data and nationally recognized installation requirements.

O'Rourke, Gerald W. "Integrated Fire Protection and HVAC Systems," *Heating/Piping/Air Conditioning*, 53:4 (April 1981), 57-61.

A review of system requirements, temperature limitations, design and installation considerations.

Schmidt, William A. "Smoke Control System Testing," *Heating/Piping/Air Conditioning*, 54:4 (April 1982), 77-81.

Discusses test considerations and emphasizes the need to develop periodic testing programs.

Semple, J. Brooks. "Smoke Control: The Retrofil Option," *Heating/Piping/Air Conditioning*, 54:4 (April 1982), 69-73.

Discussion of smoke control systems that may be used in lieu of automatic sprinkler systems. Stresses the need for working closely with an expert knowledgeable in all aspects of fire protection.

Tiskus, Alphonse T. and E.G. Dressler. "Fire Protection Planning for Cultural Institutions: Blending Risk Management, Loss Prevention, and Physical Safeguards," *Technology and Conservation*, 5:2 (Summer, 1980), 18-23.

Explains what should be evaluated as a fire hazard in a building's component parts and operations when planning for its protection.

U.S. General Services Administration. Advisory Committee on the Protection of Archives and Records. *Protecting Federal Records Centers and Archives from Fire.* Washington, DC: Govt. Print. Off., 1977. 202p.

Recommendations of a committee charged to review the state-of-the-art in protection of records, including structural design, methods of records storage, protective personnel, fire protective systems, and firefighting.

Insurance

Hamilton, John. "Insurance: Personal and Real Property," *Library Trustee Newsletter*, 1:3/4 (March-April 1978), 4-6.

Six steps to a sound insurance program: how to select insurance plans that will adequately protect library collections.

Morris, John. *The Library Disaster Preparedness Handbook.* Chicago: American Library Association, 1986. 142p.
Chapter 8, "Insurance and Risk Management" deals thoroughly with the topic.*

Morrow, Dick. "Insurance," *An Ounce of Prevention,* Toronto: Toronto Area Archivists Group Education Foundation, 1986, 90-98.
A clear discussion of insurance for libraries and archives, evaluating risks and options.*

Myers, Gerald E. *Insurance Manual for Libraries.* Chicago: American Library Association, 1977. 64p.
Covers all aspects of insurance coverage for libraries.*

Peterson, Lorna. *Risk Management for Librarians: A Bibliographical List.* Monticello, IL: Vance Bibliographies, n.d. 8p. (Public Administration Series, P-1706)
Selected bibliography.

Seal, Robert A. "Insurance for Libraries," *Conservation Administration News,* No. 19 (Oct. 1984), 8-9; No. 20 (Jan. 1985) 10-11, 26.
An excellent overview of the subject with a selective bibliography.*

Surrency, Erwin C., Wylie A. Shumm and Oscar M. Trelles. "Guarding Against Disaster," *Law Library Journal,* 66:4 (Nov. 1973), 419-428.
A sound discussion of insurance, based upon an analysis of the fire at the Temple University Law School library. Papers presented before the American Association of Law Librarians.

Trelles, O.M. "Protection of Libraries," *Law Library Journal,* 66:3 (August 1973), 241-258.
A brief history of the problems and of librarians' traditional disinterest in the topic. Covers emergency planning and includes much useful information on insurance.*

CHAPTER 6. Preservation of Library and Archival Materials

INTRODUCTION

A BUILDING IS THE HOME for the documents of our cultural and intellectual heritage. If the home is sound and well built, the items housed within it are secure. They will be preserved for present and future users. If the home is poorly constructed, they will suffer and they may be destroyed. Once a home is built, it must be maintained. The previous chapters of this book have concentrated on the construction of the library or archive building so that the materials within will be preserved. There are many decisions that can be made in the planning process that will lead to a better home for collections through the choice of materials for construction and the environmental controls that are built into it. But, once the home is built, once the library or archive opens its doors to the public, its collections must be maintained. Library and archival materials are fragile and can too easily be destroyed. This chapter will discuss the physical nature of these materials. It will suggest approaches to maintenance and housekeeping that should be adopted when the facility opens its doors. The accompanying bibliography is selective; we hope that administrators will delve further into the literature on preservation. Constructing the building is not sufficient; continued care of collections is essential or all is lost.

Preservation should be an integral part of the activity of the staff in a library or archive repository. The staff should know about the nature of the materials and how to care for them. If an institution has not established a preservation program when expansion is contemplated, this is an excellent time to do so in order to ensure that the preservation of the collections is an integral part of the planning and construction phases. The bibliography for this chapter provides a selection of basic readings on the nature of library and archival collections and how they should be maintained and preserved.

MATERIALS IN LIBRARY AND ARCHIVAL COLLECTIONS

As we have discussed, the materials found in library and archival collections are made up of matter, and all matter is impermanent. The goal of the librarian, archivist and curator is to make the materials in their care last as long as possible. This is preservation. Paper, bindings, photographs, film, video, phonograph records, computers and disks—each is susceptible to the hazards that are found in the environment where they are housed. Indeed, the "electronic library" may be more vulnerable than the traditional library of books and papers. In order to ensure an environment that is appropriate and to maintain the collections without causing unnecessary damage, it is necessary to know something about these materials.

Paper

Paper, made of vegetable fibers, was invented in the Far East, probably during the first century A.D. The fibers are beaten into a pulp. The macerated pulp is mixed with water to produce a slurry which is poured into a mold. The fibers bond together to form the sheets of paper. They are then dried, pressed to become smooth, and treated with a sizing agent so that they can be written upon. Various plants have been used to produce the fibers for paper; linen rags make the best paper, but they are expensive.

The technique of papermaking changed very little from

its inception until the late seventeenth century. Since then, a variety of techniques have been developed to speed the process. With each advance in the mechanization of papermaking, the quality of the paper was lessened to some extent. By the middle of the nineteenth century, during the 1860s, wood pulp became an effective and economical material for making paper. However, the lignin in the pulp produces an acidic reaction that literally causes the paper to react against itself. Modern sizing accelerates the problem. Thus, most paper produced in the past century is disintegrating at an unacceptably rapid rate. These papers are especially susceptible to light, dirt, air pollution, and to fluctuations in temperature and humidity, which accelerate the deterioration caused by the combination of materials within the paper itself. It is only recently that manufacturers have begun to make a better quality paper, referred to as "acid-free" (which it is not) or "permanent/durable." However, the demand for such paper is limited and the cost of retooling a paper mill to manufacture it is considerable, although the manufacturing process itself is cheaper. Nearly half of the books published in North America today are printed on acidic paper, and much of the paper that will make up future archival collections is also acidic. These materials will deteriorate; the goal of the librarian and archivist is to provide conditions for housing and storage that will retard that rate as much as possible.

There are a number of processes being developed that can retard this deterioration by removing much of the acid content in paper, then buffering the paper so that it has an alkaline reserve. This process is called deacidification. The Wei T'o process developed by engineer and librarian Richard Smith is used at the Public Archives of Canada and appears to be successful. Smaller Wei T'o units have been installed in a number of other institutions and are used to preserve special collections of research materials. However, the installation of the Wei T'o facility is only practical for institutions with a substantial body of rare or unique materials printed on acidic paper.

The Library of Congress has developed a method for deacidification using the chemical diethyl zinc, with which it plans to treat its own collections. The diethyl zinc, or DEZ, process is highly volatile and requires a specially designed facility. It is not a feasible system for libraries and archives to install, although it has potential as a service that could be offered commercially or through a regional facility. The DEZ process is now being developed by the Akzo Corporation, which will develop a facility for the treatment of the Library of Congress collections and explore how the technology can be used to treat other collections.

The British Library is working to develop a method of deacidification that will also strengthen the weakened papers, something that the Wei T'o and diethyl zinc processes cannot do. The Bibliothèque National is presently using a process similar to the Wei T'o method to deacidify its materials; other European libraries are also developing processes for deacidification and strengthening of paper. In addition, entrepreneurs in this country and abroad are also developing and testing processes with the potential to deacidify and strengthen paper at a reasonable cost. It appears that the technology for the mass treatment of embrittled collections will soon be available to all libraries and archives.

Although the technology for the deacidification and strengthening of paper is still in its infancy, it is one that every administrator should follow with considerable interest. It would be ideal if small units that can deacidify and strengthen paper and operate safely and economically were developed to be housed in libraries and archives with collections of permanent value.

Bindings

The bindings, or covers, of books are made of a variety of materials. Book covers are often called boards because they were originally made of board. Today paperboard and a variety of fabrics are used for bookbinding. Most cloth bindings bear up reasonably well. Many are made of acrylic fibers which, in the past, presented problems such as adhesion to other materials when shelved in conditions with high temperature and humidity. But today cloth bindings offer strength and durability at a reasonable price.

Leather bindings, which are usually treasured, pose particular problems, especially those produced in the nineteenth and twentieth centuries. Hides must be treated to make them pliable for binding. There were, and are, a variety of processes for the treatment of animal hides for bookbinding. Many of them cause the leather to disintegrate over time. Exposure to fluctuations in heat and humidity, air pollutants and light hasten the deterioration. Until recently, it was believed that oiling these bindings would help them keep their flexibility, but recent evidence shows that oiling can cause more harm than good and, at best, does no harm. The benefit is cosmetic and of short duration. Badly deteriorated nineteenth and twentieth century leather bindings, which suffer from a condition referred to as "red-rot," cannot be saved as they are. They can be rebound, if the inner text is reasonably sound. They can also be placed in boxes or wrapped to prevent their dirt from contaminating other materials, then placed in a closed storage area. Libraries with extensive collections of leather-bound volumes should see that they are housed under environmentally correct conditions. It is a wise decision to place them in an area designed for special collections.

Because of the fragile nature of books and bindings and the enormous, if not impossible, task of restoring them, the concept of "phase boxing" was developed at the Library of Congress and is used at a number of institutions. In principle, this means that books or collections of papers are placed in "temporary" wrappers or boxes made of acid-free materials, then placed in an environmentally sound storage area until the day when the material can be given an appropriate conservation treatment. While "phase boxing" is not meant to be forever, it is usually long-term, until mass treatments for deacidification and strengthening are readily and economically available.

Photographs

The photograph, as we know it today, is an image made from a negative printed on paper. A variety of materials have gone and continue to go into the making of a photograph. The chemicals in these materials can work upon one another and upon the paper base to hasten their deterioration. Color prints are unstable and will fade, regardless of the conditions under which they are stored. Photographic collections should be housed in environmentally controlled conditions and arranged to limit unnecessary handling. Improper housing can cause harm to photographs in a relatively short period of time.

The earliest photographic technique, the daguerreotype, has its image upon a sheet of highly polished silverplate copper. Ambrotypes are transparent thin glass negatives under which a black felt is placed to produce a positive image. The tintype is a direct positive image on a sensitized iron base. These early photographs are considered original prints because only one image could be produced, unlike a film negative which can produce a number of copies. They are particularly fragile and need to be housed in appropriate wrappers in environmentally sound conditions. They should be cleaned or otherwise treated by a photographic conservator.

Photographic collections can be housed in boxes, envelopes, and in a variety of methods that conservators have developed. The method for housing and storing these materials is best resolved with the help of a photographic conservator. A conservator is familiar with the variety of images that can be found in a collection and can help devise a storage plan that will protect the images and also work best for the use that they will receive in the institution.

Film

Motion picture film can be found in most collections. From its development by Eastman Kodak in 1899 until the late 1930s, most rolled film was made of nitrate negative stock; it was used for motion picture film and microfilm until the early 1950s. Nitrate film is extremely unstable. Stored under less than optimal conditions (cold storage with no light), it will shrink and shrivel, become tacky, soft or brittle. The images will fade and discolor into a yellow-brown shade. Finally it will emit gaseous fumes of nitric acid and will bubble and foam until it disintegrates into a fine powder. The danger is that as it deteriorates it becomes highly combustible and, if it is stored in a warm, poorly ventilated room, it can ignite spontaneously. It is also virtually impossible to extinguish since the burning film manufactures its own oxygen in the combustion process.

Most libraries do not have collections of old motion picture film, but such film does turn up. When construction is planned, collections should be checked to be sure there is none in the building. Some insurers will not cover buildings that contain nitrate film, which then must be removed from the building and disposed of by the fire department.

Nonflammable safety film replaced nitrate film by the early 1950s. Although it is safe, it also deteriorates when stored under less than ideal conditions. Modern film is made from acetate, which is less susceptible to deterioration, but it also will react adversely to environmentally unstable conditions.

Collections of motion picture films should be stored upright in boxes on metal shelves. If the film collection is circulating, it is wise to plan for an inspection station and repair area in the media department so that all films can be checked for damage when returned and minor repairs can be made.

Microforms are subject to the same hazards as films. They are more sensitive to their environment than books, and this must be taken into consideration when designing the microtext reading room. Because microtexts must be used with reading machines, and these readers can cause damage if they are broken or improperly handled, the servicing and repair of equipment and the periodic cleaning of heavily used films are important factors in planning a microtext reading room. If a collection is substantial and heavily used, it may be cost-effective to employ a full-time technician to service it. The equipment used to read microtexts is also affected by the environment in the microtext reading room; the equipment will operate best in a stable environment.

Glass slides and transparencies are another form of photographic material that is fragile and requires special care and handling. Slide collections are often heavily used. Color transparencies are unstable and their deterioration is accelerated by exposure to light. Slides can be stored in metal boxes or in books with envelope pages made of an inert polyester. They should be kept away from light when they are not used. If the library supplies slide equipment, it should be carefully maintained to curtail the damage that projection causes. Original, or archival, slides can be duplicated for use and the originals stored under the appropriate conditions. It takes careful planning to ensure that slide collections last as long as possible; one mishandling can destroy an image.

Magnetic Tape

Magnetic tape is becoming an increasingly common medium in libraries and archives. It is used for both audio and video recordings and also for computer data. It is made of a polyester base to which oxides of iron and chromium are attached. By magnetization and rearrangement of the magnetic fields borne by these oxides, a message is recorded on the tape which can be "read" by a device in the playback machine. Researchers still know too little about its stability. Magnetic media are even more sensitive to the environment than books and paper. High heat and/or humidity, or fluctuations, can cause "dropout," which is the erasure of information. The tape itself is subject to physical damage by repeated use of faulty playback equipment. It is important to periodically rewind magnetic tapes to prevent the "print through" phenomenon, which will garble the data. Smoke and particulate matter are especially destructive. Information can be lost if magnetic tapes are exposed to a magnetic field. Careful planning in the storage area will eliminate that hazard in the building.

There are a number of storage systems available for magnetic tapes. Considerable thought should be given to the storage facilities for this medium, especially for archival data. The appropriate environment is essential and it will require careful planning. Recording technology is developing rapidly. Storage sites should be visited and experts consulted. The method, or methods, of storage and housing selected will depend upon the nature and use of the collections. Cassettes afford some protection for circulating audio and video collections, but the equipment used for playback outside the library cannot be monitored. Playback equipment in the building should be kept as dust-free as possible. Regular maintenance for playback equipment is essential; manufacturer's instructions should be followed.

The technology of video and sound recording is developing rapidly, but researchers know far too little about the stability and permanence of the medium. However, much magnetic material is archival in nature and the problems that its preservation will cause must be addressed in the future.

The Computer

Today the library and archive may be to a greater or lesser degree electronic, but there is no question that the computer will play an ever more important role in every information repository. Computer technology is the most difficult information medium to discuss, because the technology is continually changing and it is difficult to know of what its physical components are made. At present most repositories have microcomputers and floppy disks. A floppy disk is a sheet of material covered with a magnetic substance (oxide) on both sides. It is burnished to prevent "drag" and other stresses, thus allowing it to withstand millions of head passes in each track. These disks are more susceptible to destruction from environmental conditions than the other materials covered in this section.

Areas that house computer facilities should be designed so that they can be kept as free of dust and pollutants as possible and cannot easily be damaged by water. The computer terminal itself is susceptible to hazards from the environment, including moisture, high or low temperatures, static electricity, dust, dirt, smoke, and power failure. Any of these conditions can cause loss of information.

Computers cannot be appended to the library or archive without considerable planning, or the resulting costs in losses can be considerable. Appropriate work areas need to be designed and maintained. The installation of computers requires special planning and design which will not only affect the immediate space in the repository, but will also affect the installation of the mechanical systems for heating, air conditioning and ventilation. The continued care of the equipment is essential. The increased use of computers in libraries and archives will have a substantial impact on the design of new buildings and on the remodeling of older structures. As writers on libraries have been pointing out for the past twenty years, the effect that computerization will have on the design of buildings is still not predictable.

THE PRESERVATION SURVEY

The time to have the staff carefully examine the needs of the collections as well as the needs of its users is immediately prior to the planning of a new or renovated building. This is the ideal time to survey the collection for conservation problems. The preservation survey will not only identify materials in poor condition; it will also clearly identify physical problems in the present facility. During the survey, members of the staff should review the condition of the collections using a scientific sampling technique. In addition to identifying materials in need of treatment, the survey will also identify problems in the building that caused the deterioration. Common causes are HVAC systems that are not designed for the needs of library and archival collections; ventilation systems that can blow dust onto the collections; light from windows or from unfiltered sources of artificial light; water pipes that occasionally leak; and flaws in the building structure itself. Restored materials should never be returned to conditions that caused the problem in the first place.

A goal of the preservation survey is to ensure that the collections are put into as good condition as possible before they are moved to new, environmentally sound quarters. The move should be accomplished with as little damage to the collections as possible. As more funds become available for the conservation of library and archival materials, it will be possible for many institutions to undertake phase boxing programs, as well as some conservation treatment for rare books and documents, during the planning and construction of a new facility.

COLLECTION MAINTENANCE

The imperfections of a building can be compensated for, in part, by the staff's concern for the collections and awareness of the factors that can cause damage. If every member of the staff understands the physical nature of the materials in the collection and participates in the planning process for the facility, he or she will be able to plan for their continued care and maintenance.

A well-trained housekeeping staff is essential. Housekeeping is important in a home. Good housekeeping is critical to the survival of library and archival collections, yet it is a mundane subject that is too frequently of little interest to the professional staff. This attitude has had an unfortunate effect on our collections. A good administrator should ensure that library and archival materials can be properly cared for in a well-designed and properly maintained repository.

Library and archival materials have to be cleaned in special ways, and the housekeeping staff cannot be expected to know them. The administrator or curator is responsible for the instruction of the housekeeping staff so that each understands how to clean and what materials to use. Every person should understand clearly why each task is to be done in a particular way. The housekeeping staff is the front line and can spot incipient problems before they become disasters. They should be encouraged to assume this responsibility and to feel that they are an integral part of the institution (which, of course, they are). The housekeeping staff in most institutions is ill-paid; often these employees have had little education; often they do not speak English well, or at all. Some continue to work in libraries, archives and museums, although they could probably make more money elsewhere, because they have a deep respect for what the materials in the collections stand for. This is something that the professional staff takes for granted or has forgotten. The professionals can see that splendid buildings are erected to house and protect the collections, but it is the housekeeping and maintenance staffs that will make them work.

Continuing housekeeping needs should be identified in the planning phase. The first step in establishing an appropriate and efficient housekeeping program is to take a careful look at the building plans and to record each task that will need to be done. The list should be long and detailed. The tasks can be grouped and consolidated, and the amount of time needed for housekeeping on a daily, weekly, monthly and annual basis can be calculated. The housekeeping plan should have an effect on the final building design. Careful planning before the building is constructed should help preserve the collections and save the institution money.

The people who are responsible for the physical plant should not only understand the working of the HVAC and other mechanical systems, but should also understand *why* it is important that these systems be maintained so that they operate properly. A breakdown in the mechanical systems can cause long-term damage to the materials in a relatively short period of time. As already mentioned, computers are particularly sensitive, and damage to them can be serious and costly. It is important for the administrator to understand this and to make it clear to the maintenance staff. Some larger libraries and archives assign a staff person to work with the physical plant personnel on a full-time basis. Even the smallest institution should have an administrator who takes responsibility for the maintenance of the building and the collections.

BIBLIOGRAPHY

Adams, Randolph G. "Librarians as Enemies of Books," *Library Quarterly*, 7 (1937), 317-331.
    A statement against the trend in librarianship toward management at the expense of the collections.

Association of Research Libraries. Office of Management Studies. *Preservation Planning Program: An Assisted Self-Study Manual for Libraries*, expanded edition prepared by Pamela W. Darling and Duane E. Webster. Washington, DC: Association of Research Libraries, 1987. 117p.
    A guide for libraries undertaking a formal study of preservation needs; covers preparation for the study, its framework, the examination of the environment and the physical condition of the collections, and disaster planning. Practical information on each phase of the self-study is provided.

Atkinson, Ross W. "Selection for Preservation: A Materialistic Approach," *Library Resources and Technical Services*, 30:4 (Oct.-Dec. 1986), 341-353.
    This article articulates a philosophy for the development of a preservation program in a library and clarifies issues that will be addressed in the conservation survey.

Baker, John P. and Marguerite C. Soroka, eds. *Library Conservation: Preservation in Perspective.* Stroudsburg, PA: Dowden, Hutchinson and Ross, 1978. 459p.

A selection of readings for librarians who must deal with problems in preservation.

Banks, Paul N. "Preservation of Library Materials," *Encyclopedia of Library and Information Science,* vol. 23. New York: Dekker, 1978, 180-222.

An excellent overview of preservation of library and archival materials covering the causes of deterioration, conservation, methods, philosophy. Bibliography.

Barrow, William J. *Deterioration of Bookstock, Causes and Remedies; Two Studies on the Permanence of Book Paper,* Randolph W. Church, ed. Richmond, VA: Virginia State Library, 1959. 70p.

Results of a major study of twentieth century book papers, funded by the Council on Library Resources.

Blades, William. *The Enemies of Books,* rev. and enl. ed. London: Elliot Stock, 1896. 196p.

A classic work, first published in 1880, that remains a relevant study on the care and preservation of library materials. An abridged version of this edition was published in *AB Bookman's Yearbook,* pt. 1, 1971, 3-22.

Clapp, Anne F. *Curatorial Care of Works of Art on Paper.* New York: Nick Lyons, 1987. 191p.

A manual covering the causes of the deterioration of paper, environmental controls and treatment procedures. Bibliography.

Cunha, George M. and Dorothy G. *Conservation of Library Materials; A Manual and Bibliography on the Care, Repair and Restoration of Library Materials,* 2nd ed. 2 vols. Metuchen, NJ: Scarecrow Press, 1971-72. 406, 414p.

Vol. 1 provides considerable information on preservation and repair; vol. 2: bibliography.

Cunha, George M. and Dorothy G. *Library and Archival Conservation: the 1980s and Beyond.* 2 vols. Metuchen, NJ: Scarecrow Press, 1983. 200, 415p.

Vol. 1 updates the history of conservation efforts and identifies current trends and needs. Vol. 2 continues the Cunhas' definitive bibliography on the conservation of library and archival materials.

Cunha, George M., Howard P. Lowell and Robert E. Schnare. *Conservation Survey Manual*. Balston Spa, NY: SMART (Section of the Management of Resources and Technology of the New York Library Association), 1982. 64p.
   An excellent manual on surveying collection needs. Included are the survey forms used by the Northeast Document Conservation Center. Bibliography and list of sources of supplies.

Fox, Lisa L. *A Core Collection in Preservation*. Chicago: American Library Association, 1988. 15p.
   An annotated bibliography of books, reports, periodicals and major articles that may prove useful in preservation planning and administration

Grove, Lee H. "Paper Deterioration—An Old Story," *College and Research Libraries*, 25:5 (Sept. 1964), 365-374.
   Discusses the efforts of librarians leading up to the studies by Barrow to deal with the problem of acid paper.

Guldbeck, Per E. *The Care of Antiques and Historical Collections*, 2nd ed., rev. and expanded by A. Bruce MacLeish. Nashville, TN: American Association for State and Local History, 1985. 248p.
   A handbook on the care, storage and handling of collections in museums, historical societies and libraries. Chapters deal with paper, leather and photographs.

Henderson, Kathryn Luther and William T., eds. *Conserving and Preserving Library Materials*. Urbana, IL: Graduate School of Library and Information Science, 1983. 207p.
   Papers from the 1981 Allerton Park Conference cover planning and establishing a preservation program.

Horton, Carolyn. *Cleaning and Preserving Bindings and Related Materials*, 2nd rev. ed. Chicago: Library Technology Program, American Library Association, 1969. 87p.
   Describes the organization and management of a systematic survey of stack conditions and a program of care for collections.

International Federation of Library Associations and Institutions. Conservation and Preservation Division. *Principles of Conservation*. Brussels, Belgium: IFLA, 1986. 25p.

The basic principles for the preservation and conservation of library and archival collections; prepared by international experts.

Lewis, Ralph H. *Manual for Museums*. Washington, DC: National Park Service, 1976. 412p.

Handbook covering all aspects of collection care.

Library Preservation Program: Models, Priorities, Possibilities, Jan Merrill-Oldham and Merrily Smith, eds. Chicago: American Library Association, 1985. 116p.

Proceedings of the first preservation conference jointly sponsored by the American Library Association and the Library of Congress in 1983. The conference was planned for library administrators and its emphasis was on organization and planning.

Lowell, Howard P. "Sources of Conservation Information for the Librarian," *Collection Management*, 4:3 (Fall 1982), 1-18.

A bibliographical discussion of the literature on library and archival conservation.

Merrill-Oldham, Jan. *Conservation and Preservation of Library Materials: A Program for the University of Connecticut Libraries*. Storrs, CT: University of Connecticut Libraries, 1984. 65p.

A comprehensive, detailed study of the care and handling of problems in a medium-sized academic library. It can serve as a working model for planning at other institutions.

Mowat, Ian R.M. "A Policy Proposal for the Conservation and Control of Bookstock in Academic Libraries," *Journal of Librarianship*, 14:4 (Oct. 1982), 266-278.

While expressing his concern for the preservation of books, the author is concerned that library materials be used and encourages better storage and security.

Nyberg, Sandra. *The Invasion of the Giant Spore*. Atlanta, GA: Southeast Library Network, Nov. 1987. 19p. (SOLINET Preservation Program Leaflet, 5)

A clearly written pamphlet outlining the causes of mold, mildew and fungi. Although chemical treatments are described, the maintenance of a clean environment is considered the critical factor in their prevention. Bibliography.

Patterson, Robert H. "Organizing for Conservation," *Library Journal*, 104:10 (May 15, 1979), 1116-1119. (Library Journal Series on Preservation, 2)
A model for libraries wanting to develop a broad-based program with administrative support.

Pederson, Ann, ed. *Keeping Archives*. Sydney: Australian Society of Archivists, Inc., 1987. 374p.
An introductory manual for archivists providing practical guidelines for archival management. Conservation and preservation are emphasized throughout the text. Chapter 8, "Conservation," by Michael Piggott, pp. 219-252, is basic and thorough in its discussion of preservation and conservation considerations.

Petherbridge, Guy, ed. *Conservation of Library and Archive Materials and the Graphic Arts*. London: Butterworths, 1987. 328p.
Technical papers on the nature of books and paper and their conservation. Proceedings of an International Conference held in Cambridge, England, in 1980, which brought together experts to address the problems faced by librarians and archivists.

Preservation of Historical Records. Washington, DC: National Academy Press, 1986. 108p.
Report of the Committee on Preservation of Historical Records, the National Materials Advisory Board, and the Commission on Engineering and Technical Systems, National Research Council, brought together to study the methods available for the preservation of materials housed in the National Archives. Various methods for preserving paper records are examined and alternative actions for preservation are assessed.

Ritzenthaler, Mary Lynn. *Archives and Manuscripts: Conservation; A Manual on Physical Care and Management*, rev. ed. Chicago: Society of American Archivists, 1984. 151p.
An essential guide for administrators; addresses problems and issues and offers some solutions to the problems in preserving collections. Bibliography.

Smith, Richard D. "Guidelines for Preservation," *Special Libraries*, 59:5 (May-June 1968), 346-352.
Discusses the causes of paper deterioration and recommends that each library and archive establish a written preservation policy.

Smolian, Steven. "Preservation, Deterioration and Restoration of Recording Tape," *ARSC* (Association for Recorded Sound Collections) *Journal*, 19:2/3 (1987), 37-53
Thorough discussion of the problems faced in attempting to preserve recorded tape, with suggestions for storage and housing.

Swartzburg, Susan Garretson. *Preserving Library Materials: A Manual*. 2nd ed. Metuchen, NJ: Scarecrow Press. Forthcoming.
A basic guide to the problems and preservation of library materials. Bibliography; glossary.

Swartzburg, Susan Garretson, ed. *Conservation in the Library*. Westport, CT: Greenwood Press, 1983. 234p.
A manual, with chapters contributed by experts, on the care, handling and storage of materials found in libraries and archives. Bibliography.

Thomson, Garry. "Impermanence—Some Chemical and Physical Aspects," *Museums Journal*, 64:1 (June 1964), 16-36.
Discusses chemical changes in the museum environment, the movement of water in organic material, and concludes that much research on "permanence" needs to be done.

Wilson, Alex. "For This and Future Generations: Managing the Conflict Between Conservation and Use," *Library Review*, 31 (Autumn 1982), 163-172.
The author discusses the harm to collections due to the neglect by librarians and the economic cost of that neglect; a call to action.

Winger, Howard W. and Richard D. Smith, eds. *Deterioration and Preservation of Library Materials*. Chicago: University of Chicago Press, 1970. 200p.
Covers all aspects of preservation, with bibliographical notes. See especially "Environmental Factors Affecting the Permanence of Library Materials," by Carl J. Wessell, pp. 39-84.

Papers presented at the 34th annual conference of the Graduate Library School, University of Chicago.

Word, Philip R. "Conservation: Keeping the Past Alive," *Museum*, 34:1 (1982), 6-9.
   A statement of what conservation is, including environmental control and storage.

APPENDIXES

APPENDIX I. Case Studies

THE PROFESSIONAL LITERATURE is replete with case studies on the planning, design, and construction of library and archive buildings. Nearly every administrator will be responsible for the planning of a new facility or the remodeling of an older structure in the course of his or her professional career—and nearly every administrator has a compulsion to write about that experience. The lack of training librarians and archivists receive in the planning and design of buildings is evident when reviewing the literature. The bulk of the case studies are descriptive; many are accompanied by plans, schematic drawings and photographs. However, they are, in the main, singularly unhelpful. Those few library and archive administrators with excellent knowledge of spatial relations and some background in construction might find this pictorial material of some use, but it is our experience that few administrators can "read" three-dimensionally. Although the ability to read plans and drawings is certainly a useful skill, many administrators will need to rely on detailed, carefully prepared programs, and then "stay on top of it." Many will gain the ability to read the plans and drawings more easily as the project progresses. Some will not, and this need not hinder the process.

When this volume was initially planned, the intent was to include a chapter on the best buildings that have been planned and built in the past few decades, with critiques from the professional literature and illustrations. It soon became evident that the number of successful library and archive buildings might be counted on one hand, if one were generous. We then hoped to direct the reader to cogent critiques of buildings, but we found that we could turn to only two librarians for solid, published criticism: David Kaser and Ellsworth Mason. Both are experienced building consultants with keen eyes and facile pens. *Mason on Library Buildings*, a collection of his works, published in 1980, should be required reading for every librarian and archivist. Kaser's critique of the Wells College library and his review of postwar library architecture, both of which appeared in *College and Research Libraries*, are excellent.

The selected bibliography that follows cites articles that have been published over the past forty years in the hope that they will be helpful to the planner. However, there is no question that the best "case studies" are to be found through visits to recently completed library and archive repositories. There one can see the successes and the failures of a building and talk to the personnel involved with its planning and construction.

BIBLIOGRAPHY

Association des archivistes et bibliothécaires de Belgique. *La Construction et l'Amenagement des Bibliothèques et Depots d'Archives*, ed. G. Braive and D. Hanappe. Brussels: 1973. 114p. French
    Discusses planned libraries and archive repositories with the preservation of materials a serious consideration.

Beach, Robert F. and Walter H. Martin. "Union Theological Seminary Air Conditions Its Library," *College and Research Libraries*, 18:4 (July 1957), 297-302.
    The air conditioning of a research collection with the premise that it is good for people and for the preservation of the materials.

"The Beinecke Rare Book and Manuscript Library, a Statement by the Architects, Skidmore, Owings and Merrill," *Yale University Library Gazette*, 38:4 (April 1964), 127-130.
    A description of the library by the architects, who emphasize the care and preservation of the collections in what has proven a difficult structure for their physical maintenance.

Castle, Paul. "Five University Libraries: a Comparative Study," *Architects' Journal,* 147:10 (March 6, 1968), 561-577.
A study of the libraries at Edinburgh, Warwick, York, Lancaster, and Essex in terms of size; environmental conditions for books, readers, and staff; and extent of flexibility for future expansion.

Conger, Lucinda. "The Annex Library of Princeton University: The Development of a Compact Storage Library," *College and Research Libraries,* 31:3 (May 1970), 160-168.
A description of the planning and operation of the library's off-site storage facility.

David, Charles W. "Postwar Plans for a University Library Building," *College and Research Libraries,* 6:2 (March 1945), 112-118.
A review of the plan for the University of Pennsylvania library with its emphasis on air conditioning, because of the local climate, and a concern for stacks that fill too rapidly.

Deitch, Joseph. "Portrait: Paul Goldberger," *Wilson Library Bulletin,* 62:5 (Jan. 1987), 54-57.
Goldberger, winner of the Pulitzer Prize for distinguished architectural criticism, discusses American library architecture.*

Ferguson, David J. "Designing for Fire and Safety: The Development of Suitable Systems for an Underground Museum," *Technology and Conservation,* 7:4 (Winter 1982), 26-30.
The fire protection system and the fire prevention aspects in the design of the underground addition to the Smithsonian Institution are described.*

Hutton, Brian. "The Planning of an Archives Building: Public Records Office of Northern Ireland," *Irish Archives Bulletin,* 2:2 (1972), 14-19.
Discusses the special problems of designing archive repositories as distinct from libraries, and provides brief guidelines for planning.

Kaser, David. "Twenty-Five Years of Academic Library Building Planning," *College and Research Libraries,* 45:4 (July 1984), 268-281.
An excellent critical article that discusses the evolution of

the modular design concept over the past 25 years, observing that it originally lent itself well to efficient library operations. However, modifications, such as atria, designer lighting, monumental effects, unusual shapes, and other devices, work to the detriment of library service and create problems with the building's environment.*

Langmead, Stephen and Margaret Beckman. *New Library Design: Guide Lines to Planning Academic Library Buildings.* Toronto: Wiley, 1970. 117p. Illus.

Recommendations based upon the authors' experience in planning and building the award-winning University of Guelph library. In his introduction, Guy Sylvestre, the former National Librarian of Canada, comments, "The new philosophy of librarianship, which puts the accent on communication rather than it does on conservation, is unavoidably reflected in a new approach to library buildings."

Lodewycks, K.A. *Essentials of Library Planning.* Melbourne, Aust.: University of Melbourne Library, 1961. 136p.

This book is based on the author's experience in planning the Baillieu Library, Melbourne University. A good planning document with sound advice and a concern for the protection of library materials, although some of the advice on preservation is now dated.

Mason, Ellsworth. *Mason on Library Buildings.* Metuchen, NJ: Scarecrow Press, 1980. 333p.

A collection of the author's critical articles on the planning of library buildings, and his cogent criticism of a number of those structures. Mason's purpose is to present American practice in library planning, and he teaches the reader a great deal about what is good and what is bad planning. The buildings reviewed include Beinecke Library, Yale University; Rockefeller Library, Brown University; Countway Library of Medicine, Harvard University; Dalhousie University Library; Robarts Library, University of Toronto; and Sedgewick Undergraduate Library, University of British Columbia. The essays are updated from their original publication and the notes accompanying them are especially interesting and informative.*

Streit, Samuel A. and Roberta G. Sautter. "Brown Renovates for Preservation," *Conservation Administration News,* no. 10 (July 1982), 1-4.

An analysis of the renovation of a Carnegie building to provide a modern research facility, preserving the best of the old.*

"Technology Trends: Keeping Cool . . . Not Hot, Cruel World for Museum's Collections," *Technology and Conservation,* 4:1 (Spring 1979), 5-8.
Discussion of the environmental factors considered for the preservation of the collections when the I.M. Pei Group designed the East Wing of the National Gallery.

Wright, William C. "The New Jersey State Records Storage Center," *Conservation Administration News,* no. 15 (Oct. 1983), 1-4.
A description of a carefully planned records storage facility. The shelves collapsed just after the article was written because the stack configuration was improperly tested and was unable to bear the weight of the materials stored on them.

APPENDIX II. Bibliography of Bibliographies

D URING THE COURSE OF the preparation of this book, the authors consulted a variety of bibliographies on architecture, construction, preservation, and related topics. We hope that our readers will explore them, as we have done, for they can provide references for specific information that we have not included in our selective bibliography.

Banks, Paul N. *A Selective Bibliography on the Conservation of Research Library Materials.* Chicago: Newberry Library, 1981. Numbered by section.
An extensive bibliography, without annotations. One section is devoted to library and archive buildings.

Bradfield, Valerie J., ed. *Information Sources in Architecture.* London: Butterworths, 1983. 419p. (Butterworths Guides to Information Sources)
A guide to the sources and nature of information available on architecture and construction; attempts to review the coverage of information over the whole of the construction process.

Cowgill, Clinton H. and George E. Pettengill. *The Library Building.* Washington, DC: American Institute of Architects, 1959. (AIA Building Type Reference Guide BTRG 3-3)
An extensive bibliography compiled by the AIA librarian.

Cunha, George M. and Dorothy G. *Conservation of Library Materials; A Manual and Bibliography on the Care, Repair and Restoration of Library Materials,* 2nd ed. Vol. 2: *Bibliography.* Metuchen, NJ: Scarecrow Press, 1972. 412p.
An extensive bibliography covering all aspects of the preservation of library and archival materials.

Cunha, George M. and Dorothy G. *Library and Archives Conservation: the 1980s and Beyond.* Vol. 2: *Bibliography.* Metuchen, NJ: Scarecrow Press, 1984. 415 p.

This bibliography continues where the volume listed above left off. It is an invaluable resource.

Dahlgren, Andres C. and Erla P. Heyns, comp. *Planning Library Buildings: A Select Bibliography.* Chicago: Library Administration and Management Association, American Library Association. 1990. 60p.

Covers all aspects of planning and design for all types of libraries. Not annotated.

Dale, Doris Cruger. *Two-year Community and Junior College Library Buildings: A Bibliography of Books, Articles, and Research Studies.* Monticello, IL: Vance Bibliographies, June 1982. 27p. (A-747)

Covers material published between 1960 and 1980.

Duchein, Michel, comp. *Basic International Bibliography of Archive Administration.* New York: Saur, 1978. 250p. (*Archivum*, 25)

Bibliography covering all aspects of archives administration. "Conservation and Restoration of Archives," pp. 128-153, covers general studies, buildings and equipment, conservation, and security matters. Publication sponsored by the International Council on Archives.

Eisenbeis, Kathleen and Carson Holloway. "Building or Renovating Libraries: A Bibliography of Government Documents," *North Carolina Libraries*, 39:3 (Fall 1981), 42-48.

A selected list of government publications concerning standards and current practices in architecture for public buildings. Emphasis on documents to assist the librarian as a member of the planning team. Covers law and regulations on a state and federal level, efficient energy use, historic preservation, and general publications.

Fox, Lisa L. *A Core Collection in Preservation.* Chicago: Resources and Technical Services Division, American Library Association, 1988. 15p.

Annotated bibliography of books, reports, periodicals, and major articles useful for preservation planning and administration.

Godel, Jules B. *Sources of Construction Information.* Vol. 1: *Books.* Metuchen, NJ: Scarecrow Press, 1977. 661p.

An annotated guide to reports, books, periodicals, standards and codes; covers major sources of information, planning, management, materials, the construction industry, fire protection, safety and security.

Gretes, Frances C. *Directory of International Periodicals and Newsletters on the Built Environment.* New York: Van Nostrand Reinhold, 1986. 175p.

Bibliography listing over 1,200 periodicals and newsletters dealing with the built environment. Provides full bibliographical information and alphabetic, subject and geographic indices.

Harris, Michael H. and Donald G. Davis, Jr. *American Library History: A Bibliography.* Austin, TX: University of Texas Press, 1978. 260p.

Over 3,000 references to articles and books on American libraries and related areas published through 1976.

Hunter, John E. *Security for Museums and Historic Houses: An Annotated Bibliography.* Nashville, TN: American Association for State and Local History, 1975. 8p. (Technical Leaflet 83; *History News,* 30:5, May 1975)

A short, selective bibliography on prevention and detection of security violations.

Melynk, A. "Architecture of Academic Libraries in Europe: Bibliography, 1960-1970," *College and Research Libraries,* 33:3 (May 1972), 228-235.

Bibliography with general studies and arrangement by country.

Morrow, Carolyn Clark and Stephen B. Schoenly. *A Conservation Bibliography for Librarians, Archivists, and Administrators.* Troy, NY: Whitson, 1979. 271p.

Bibliography of books and articles published between 1966 and 1978, with emphasis on paper conservation. Not annotated.

Murray, Toby. "Bibliography on Disasters, Disaster Preparedness and Disaster Recovery," *Disaster Planning: Preparedness and Recovery for Libraries and Archives,* by Sally A. Buchanan. Paris: UNESCO, 1988, 139-182.

Comprehensive bibliography; not annotated.

National Trust for Historic Preservation. *Annotated List of Newsletters on Historic Preservation and Related Subjects.* Washington, DC: National Trust for Historic Preservation, July 1979. 19p.
Newsletters on historic preservation focusing on national issues. Compiled by the National Trust library.

Oehlerts, Donald E. "Sources for the Study of American Library Architecture," *Journal of Library History,* 11:1 (Jan. 1976), 66-78.
Gives sources of information as well as bibliography.

Rath, Frederick A. *A Bibliography on Historical Organization Practices.* Vol. 2: *Care and Conservation of Collections,* R.S. Reese, comp. Nashville, TN: American Association for State and Local History, 1977. 107p.
Selective bibliography with some annotations. See especially Chapter 5, "Environmental Factors in Conservation."

Sable, Martin H. "The Protection of the Library and Archive: An International Bibliography," *Library and Archival Security,* 5:2/3 (Summer/Fall 1983), 1-183.
International in scope. Arranged chronologically by topic, without annotations. Covers disasters, fire and flooding, theft, insurance, etc.

Shaw, Thomas Shuler, comp. *Library Architecture: A Selected and Annotated List of References with Emphasis on the Planning of Large Libraries.* Washington, DC: Library of Congress General Reference and Bibliographic Division, June 1955. 35p. (Typescript)
Covers bibliographies, general works, types of libraries, equipment and furnishings, interiors, lighting, heating and ventilation, and other topics.

Smith, John F. *A Critical Bibliography of Building Conservation.* London: Mansell, 1978. 207p.
An attempt to cover all important material published up to 1976 with 2,238 annotated entries arranged by subject. Emphasis on the conservation of historic buildings.

Snowball, George J. and Rosemary Thomson, comp. *Planning College and University Library Buildings: A Select Bibliography,* 2nd ed. Chicago: American Library Association, Library

Administration and Management Association, Buildings and Equipment Section, Buildings for College and University Libraries Committee, 1984. 42p.
A bibliography with no annotations; indexed by author, title and library/institution.

Stephenson, Mary Sue. *Planning Library Facilities: A Selected, Annotated Bibliography*. Metuchen, NJ: Scarecrow Press, 1990. 249p.
Over 800 entries for materials concerned with the planning, design and evaluation of library buildings, published between 1970 and 1988. Annotated.

Stromeyer, Rainald. *Europaische Bibliotheksbauten seit 1930*. Wiesbaden: Harrassowitz, 1962, 147-172.
A bibliography of 553 references, mostly in German, with emphasis on European libraries.

Swartzburg, Susan G. "Basic Preservation Bibliography," *Conservation Administration News*, No. 44 (Jan. 1991), 10-12.
Basic texts on preservation and conservation; in print in 1990.

Taylor, Thomas H. Jr. and Christopher A. Sowick. *Publications of the National Bureau of Standards Relative to Building Technology*. Part 1: *1901-June 30, 1960*. Ottawa: Association for Preservation Technology, 1980. 120p.
Annotated bibliography with subject index of research undertaken by the National Bureau of Standards. Guide to twentieth century building materials and system performance.

Treese, William L. *Library Security*. Iowa City, IA: Art Libraries Society/North America, 1980. 14p.
An annotated bibliography; selective and limited primarily to post-1978 publications. Covers general material, electronic security and surveillance, building design, insurance, motivation for theft, and prevention.

Vance, Mary A. *Book Conservation and Restoration: A Bibliography*. Monticello, IL: Vance Bibliographies, May 1981. 8 p. (Architecture Series, Bibliography A-483)
An interesting compilation with government reports and a number of references for foreign books and articles on the subject of conservation and environmental problems.

Vance, Mary A. *Dampness in Buildings: A Revision of A-500.* Monticello, IL: Vance Bibliographies, 1986. 18p. (Architecture Series, Bibliography A-1591)
  Over 100 references, without annotations, by author, title and key word.

Weis, Ina J. *The Design of Library Areas and Buildings; A Bibliography.* Monticello, IL: Vance Bibliographies, Jan. 1981. 80p. (A413).
  An extensive bibliography.

Wood, Kate. "Library Planning: An Annotated Bibliography," *Library and Information Bulletin* (Library Association), no. 24 (1974), 4-18.
  An update of "Library Planning and Building: An Annotated Select Bibliography," published in 1967. International in scope; includes all aspects of planning, but excludes case studies. Information based upon sources available in the Library Association library.

APPENDIX III. Bibliography of Journals

THE FOLLOWING JOURNALS often carry information on planning new library buildings, renovating old ones, as well as case studies of completed projects. The journals in the field of preservation/conservation also have articles that can prove to be very helpful in the planning process.

The majority of these journals are listed in the *Directory of International Periodicals and Newsletters on the Built Environment*, by Frances C. Gretes (New York: Van Nostrand Reinhold, 1986), a comprehensive, annotated bibliography that will provide more specialized references. The production of this list was greatly facilitated by this excellent reference work.

ASHRAE Journal
  monthly, 1959 +
ASHRAE Transactions
American Society of Heating, Refrigeration and Air
    Conditioning Engineers
1791 Tullie Circle, N.E.
Atlanta, GA 30329
  2 volumes per year

The Abbey Newsletter
Ellen McCrady, Editor
320 East Center
Provo, UT 84601
  6/year, 1975 +

Air Conditioning, Heating and Refrigeration News
Business News Publishing Company

P.O. Box 2600
Troy, MI 48007
  weekly, 1926 +

American Concrete Institute Journal
P.O. Box 19150, Redford Station
Detroit, MI 48219
  bi-monthly, 1929 +

American Institute for Conservation Journal
1400 16th Street, N.W., Suite 340
Washington, DC 20036
  biannual, 1960 +.

American School and University
North American Publishing Company
401 North Broad Street
Philadelphia, PA 19108
  monthly, 1928 +

Architects' Journal
Architectural Press, Ltd.
9 Queen Ann's Gate
London, SW1H 9BY, England
  weekly, 1894 +

Architectural Design
42 Leinster Gardens
London W2 3AN, England
  monthly, 1930 +

Architectural Record
McGraw-Hill Information Systems Company
1221 Avenue of the Americas
New York, NY 10020
  bi-weekly, 1891 +

Architectural Technology
A.I.A. Service Corporation
1735 New York Avenue, N.W.
Washington, DC 20006
  quarterly, 1983 +

Architecture
(formerly *A.I.A. Journal*)
American Institute of Architects
1735 New York Avenue, N.W.
Washington, DC 20006
  monthly, 1944 +

Building
Building Services Publications, Ltd.
Builder House
1-3 Pemberton Row
London EC4P 4H2, England
  weekly, 1842 +

Building Design and Construction
Cahners Publishing Company
475 Park Avenue South
New York, NY 10016
  monthly, 1958 +

Buildings
Stamats Communications, Inc.
427 Sixth Street, S.E.
Cedar Rapids, IA 52406
  monthly, 1906 +

Codes and Standards
Kelly P. Reynolds & Associates, Inc.
2624 North Troy Street
Chicago, IL 60647
  monthly, 1980 +

Commercial Renovation
(Formerly *Commercial Remodeling*)
David Sauer
8 South Michigan Avenue
Chicago, IL 60603
  bi-monthly, 1979 +

Communique
Association for Preservation Technology
Box 2487, Station D

Ottawa, Ontario K1P 5W6, Canada
   bi-monthly, 1972 +

Conservation Administration News
McFarlin Library
University of Tulsa
600 South College
Tulsa, OK 74104
   quarterly, 1979 +

Conservation News
United Kingdom Institute for Conservation
Tate Gallery
Millbank
London SW1P 4RG, England
   3/year, 1975 +

Durability of Building Materials
Elsevier Scientific Publishing Company
Box 211
1000 AE Amsterdam, Netherlands
   quarterly, 1982 +

Electric Comfort Conditioning News
Electrical Information Publications, Inc.
2132 Fordem Avenue
Madison, WI 53704
   monthly, 1957 +

Energy and Buildings
Elsevier Science Publications
655 Avenue of the Americas
New York, NY 10010
   quarterly, 1977 +

Facilities Planning News
115 Orinda Way
Orinda, CA 94563
   bi-monthly, 1982 +

Fire Journal
National Fire Protection Association
Batterymarch Park

Quincy, MA 02269
    bi-monthly, 1907 +

Heating/Piping/Air Conditioning
Reinhold Publishing Division
600 Summer Street
Stamford, CT 06904
    monthly, 1929 +

I.C.O.M.O.S. Bulletin
International Council on Monuments and Sites
Hotel Saint-Aignan
75 Rue du Temple
75003 Paris, France
    annual, 1985 +

Library and Archival Security
(Formerly *Library Security Newsletter*)
Haworth Publications
149 Fifth Avenue
New York, NY 10010
    3/year, 1975 +

Library Journal
Bowker Magazine Group
Cahners Magazine Division
248 West 17th Street
New York, NY 10011
    20/year, 1876 +
The December 1 issue is devoted to Library Design and
    Construction

Lighting Design and Application
Illuminating Society of North America
345 East 47th Street
New York, NY 10017
    monthly, 1906 +

Museum
UNESCO
7-9 Place de Fontenoy
75700 Paris, France

or
UNIPUB
Box 1222
Ann Arbor, MI 48106
  monthly, 1948 +

Museum News
American Association of Museums
1055 Thomas Jefferson Street, N.W.
Washington, DC 20007
  bi-monthly, 1924 +

*Restaurator; International Journal for the Preservation of
    Library and Archival Materials*
Munksgaard International Publishers, Ltd.
35, Norre Sogade
DK-1370 Copenhagen K, Denmark
  irregular, 1969 +

Security Systems Administration
101 Crossways Park West
Woodbury, NY 11797
  monthly

Security World
Security World Publishing Company
2639 South La Cienega Boulevard
Los Angeles, CA 90034
  monthly, 1964 +

Studies in Conservation
International Institute for Conservation
6 Buckingham Street
London WC2N 6BA, England
  quarterly, 1952 +

Technology and Conservation
Technology Organization, Inc.
One Emerson Place
Boston, MA 02114
  irregular, 1975 +

APPENDIX IV. Directory of Organizations

READING EDUCATES THE MIND; however, talking to people can help us gain confidence. As librarians, archivists and curators, we are faced with the task of a negotiator. We meet with professionals who plan the areas in which we are obliged to work. It is, therefore, our responsibility to keep them on track, to try to understand their point of view, but more importantly, to educate them with regard to our needs. Being aware of the professional groups and associations that can provide help increases our base of knowledge.

Once you are ready to develop a new environment, take note of the following associations and organizations which can provide considerable information during the planning and construction processes and for the long-term operation of a facility.

American Association for State and Local History (AASLH)
172 Second Avenue, North, Suite 102
Nashville, TN 37204
  (615) 255-2971

American Association of Museums (AAM)
P.O. Box 33399
Washington, DC 20053
  (202) 338-5300

American Concrete Institute (ACI)
P.O. Box 19150
Detroit, MI 48219
  (313) 532-2600

American Institute for the Conservation of Artistic and
    Historic Works (AIC)
1400 16th Street, N.W. Suite 340
Washington, DC 20036
    (202) 232-6636

American Institute of Architects (AIA)
1735 New York Avenue, N.W.
Washington, DC 20006
    (202) 626-7494

American Library Association (ALA)
50 East Huron Street
Chicago, IL 60611
    (312) 944-2433 / (800) 545-2433
    Association of College and Research Libraries (ACRL), Rare
        Books and Manuscripts Section (RBMS)
    Association for Library Collections and Technical Services
        (ALCTS), Preservation of Library Materials Section (PLMS)
    Library Administration & Management Association (LAMA),
        Buildings & Equipment Section

American National Standards Institute (ANSI)
1430 Broadway
New York, NY 10018
    (212) 354-3300

American Society for Testing and Materials (ASTM)
1916 Race Street
Philadelphia, PA 19103
    (215) 299-5400

American Society of Heating, Refrigerating and Air Condition-
    ing Engineers (ASHRAE)
1791 Tullie Circle, N.E.
Atlanta, GA 30329
    (404) 636-8400

American Society of Mechanical Engineers (ASME)
345 East 47th Street
New York, NY 10017
    (212) 705-7722

Associated General Contractors of America, Inc.
1957 E Street, N.W.
Washington, DC 20006
  (202) 393-2040

Building Officials Conference of America (BOCA)
4051 West Flossmoor Road
Country Club Hills, IL 60477
  (312) 799-2300

Canadian Conservation Institute (CCI)
1030 Innes Road
Ottawa, Ontario K1A OM8, Canada
  (613) 998-3721

Canadian Museum Association
Resource Center
280 Metcalfe Street
Ottawa, Ontario K2P 1R7, Canada
  (613) 233-5653

Conservation Center for Art and Historic Artifacts (CCAHA)
264 South 23rd Street
Philadelphia, PA 19102
  (215) 545-0613

Environmental Protection Agency (EPA)
401 M Street, S.W.
Washington, DC 20460
  (202) 382-4700

Illuminating Engineering Society of North America
345 East 47th Street
New York, NY 10017
  (212) 705-7926

International Centre for the Study of the Preservation and the
    Restoration of Cultural Property (ICCROM)
13 via di San Michele
00153 Rome, Italy

International Council of Museums (ICOM)
Conservation Committee
c/o American Association of Museums
(see above)

International Council on Archives (ICA)
60 Rue des Frances-Bourgois
F-75003 Paris, France

International Federation of Library Associations and
    Institutions (IFLA)
Central Secretariat
Netherlands Congress Building
P.O.B. 82128
2508EC The Hague, Netherlands

International Institute for the Conservation of Artistic
    & Historic Works (IIC)
6 Buckingham Street
London WC2N 6BA, England

National Institute of Standards and Technology
Gaithersburg, MD 20899
    (301) 975-2000

National Fire Protection Association (NFPA)
Batterymarch Park
Quincy, MA 02269
    (800) 344-3555

National Information Standards Organization—Z39 (NISO)
National Institute of Standards and Technology
Administration 101, E106
Gaithersburg, MD 20899
    (301) 975-2814; FAX (301) 975-2128

National Institute for Conservation (NIC)
3299 K Street, N.W., Suite 403
Washington, DC 20007
    (202) 625-1495

National Preservation Program Office (NPPO)
Library of Congress
Washington, DC 20540
  (202) 287-1840

National Roofing Contractors Association
6250 River Road
Rosemont, IL 60018
  (312) 318-6722

New York State Conservation Consultancy
2199 Saw Mill River Road
Elmsford, NY 10523
  (914) 592-6726

Northeast Document Conservation Center (NEDCC)
100 Brickstone Square
Andover, MA 01810
  (508) 470-1010

Occupational Safety and Health Administration (OSHA)
U.S. Department of Labor
Washington, DC 20210
  (202) 634-7960

Society of American Archivists (SAA)
600 South Federal Street, Suite 504
Chicago, IL 60605
  (312) 922-0140

Society of Architectural Historians (SAH)
1700 Walnut Street, Suite 716
Philadelphia, PA 19103
  (215) 235-0224

Southeast Library Network, Inc. (SOLINET)
Preservation Program
1201 Peachtree Street, N.E.
Plaza Level, 400 Colony Square
Atlanta, GA 30361
  (800) 999-8558

Special Libraries Association (SLA)
1700 Eighteenth Street, N.W.
Washington, DC 20009
  (202) 234-4700

Technology and Conservation
One Emerson Place
Boston, MA 02114
  (617) 227-8581

Underwriters Laboratories, Northbrook (UL)
333 Pfingsten Road
Northbrook, IL 60062
  (312) 272-8800

UNESCO—ICOM Museum Documentation Centre
Maison de l'Unesco
1 Rue Miollis
F-75732 Paris, France

Index

215

Author Index